Tampa Review 53

❖ A GALLERY OF LITERARY AND VISUAL ART IN PRINT FOR 52 YEARS ❖

Tampa Review is published twice each year by the University of Tampa Press. Founded in 1964 as *UT Poetry Review*, *Tampa Review* is the oldest continuously published literary journal in Florida. Subscriptions in the United States are $25 per year; basic subscription is the same outside the U.S., but write for mailing cost by surface mail. Payment should be made by money order or check payable in U.S. funds. International airmail rates are available and vary; write for specific information. Subscription copies not received will be replaced without charge only if notice of nonreceipt is given by subscribers within six months following publication.

Editorial and business correspondence should be addressed to *Tampa Review*, The University of Tampa, 401 West Kennedy Boulevard, Tampa, Florida 33606-1490. Manuscripts and queries must be accompanied by a stamped, self-addressed envelope. Manuscripts are read only during September, October, November, and December. See submission guidelines at http://tampareview.ut.edu

Copyright © 2016 by University of Tampa Press. All rights reserved.
International Standard Serial Number (ISSN) 0896-064X
ISBN 978-1-59732-143-3

Tampa Review is indexed by *Index of American Periodical Verse* (Metuchen, N.J.: Scarecrow Press), *Annual Bibliography of English Language and Literature* (Cambridge, England: Modern Humanities Research Association), *POEMFINDER* (CD-ROM Poetry Index), *The American Humanities Index* (Albany, N.Y.: Whitston Publishing), and the *MLA International Bibliography*. Member of the Council of Literary Magazines and Presses (CLMP), Council of Editors of Learned Journals (CELJ), and the Florida Literary Arts Coalition (FLAC).

The editors gratefully acknowledge the generous assistance of David Connelly, Director of Public Relations; Katherine Pill, Curator of Contemporary Art; and Bridget Bryson, Manager of Curatorial Affairs and Digital Projects, Museum of Fine Arts, St. Petersburg, who made it possible to include the art from *Our America: The Latino Presence in American Art* on view at the Museum of Fine Arts, St. Petersburg, October 27, 2017-January 22, 2017. *The Dominican York* by Scherezade Garcia, reproduced on our cover, was part of the *Our America* tour but was temporarily unavailable for showing in St. Petersburg. Additional thanks to the Smithsonian American Art Museum and its suppporters for organizing the exhibition and for permission to reproduce selected pieces in this issue.

Typography and design by Richard Mathews

Printed on acid free paper ∞

Manufactured in the United States of America

**For additional information visit *Tampa Review* at
http://tampareview.ut.edu**

Editor

Richard Mathews

Fiction Editors

**Andrew Plattner
Yuly Restrepo**

Nonfiction Editor

Daniel Dooghan

Poetry Editor

Elizabeth Winston

Editorial Assistants

**Sean Donnelly
Joshua Steward**

Staff Assistant

Josie Bready

Published by the

University of Tampa Press

Tampa Review 53

ON THE COVER: Scherezade García, *The Dominican York*, from the series *Island of Many Gods*, 2006, acrylic, charcoal, ink, and sequins on paper, Smithsonian American Art Museum, Museum purchase made possible by the R. P. Whitty Company and the Cooperating Committee on Architecture © 2006, Scherezade García.

This intriguing image of a saintly child combines elements of the old and new into an eloquent contemporary icon. There is an echo of the portrait heads of saints that could adorn the walls of a chapel, but the halo involves what might be traces of jet trails on the sky or the wakes of dolphins or manatees through water, or circling giant mosquitoes. The color choice of background might be the blue of Caribbean seas and tinges of seaweed, or a shaded daylight portrait beneath an island sky, with hints of moss, or mold. Born in Santo Domingo, Dominican Republic, García is a founding member of the printmaking collective Dominican York Proyecto Grafica, a group of artists of Dominican descent who live and work in the New York City area. She says that her "work inhabits a baroque universe of different worlds of aesthetics planes" and mentions her attraction to "the inversion of traditional beliefs of salvation, and the questioning of religious and social uses of the notion of paradise."

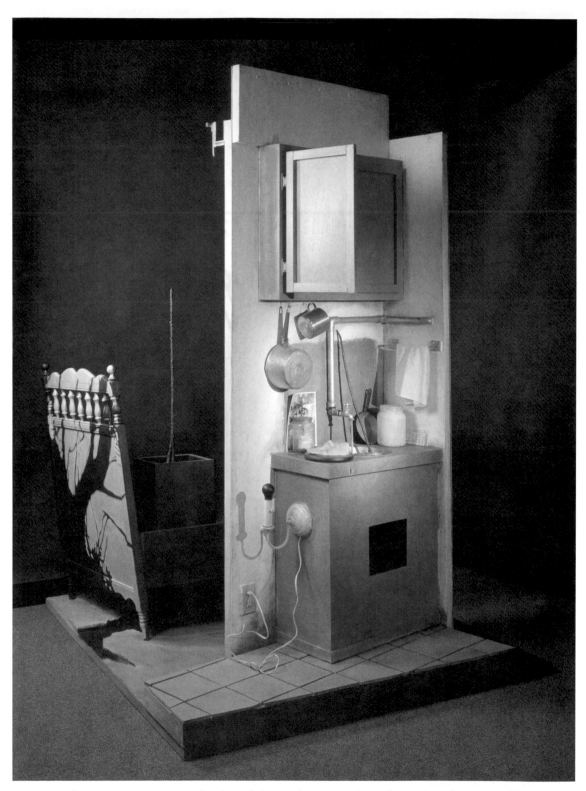

María Brito, *El Patio de Mi Casa*, 1990, mixed media, including acrylic paint, wood, wax, latex, gelatin silver prints and found objects, Smithsonian American Art Museum, Museum purchase through the Smithsonian Institution Collections Acquisition Program. © 1991, María Brito. Reproduced courtesy of Museum of Fine Arts, St. Petersburg, from "Our America: The Latino Presence in American Art."

Please Repeat My Name

The refrigerator arrived as a belated birthday present from an uncle who usually sent nothing. Audrey had to wait at the post office to claim it, after a series of notices were left on her door. She stood in line one morning in her strangely colored winter coat with all the people buying money orders. She held the latest notice.

WE HAVE MADE SEVERAL ATTEMPTS, it read. WE ARE UNABLE TO DELIVER YOUR PACKAGE. WE WOULD LIKE TO CONTINUE ATTEMPTING. BUT WE CANNOT. WE ARE LEGALLY UNABLE TO PROVIDE APOLOGIES ALTHOUGH WE WOULD LIKE TO. IN THE MEANTIME YOUR PACKAGE IS BEING HELD AT THE POST OFFICE.

She tore off the wrapping. *Personal* refrigerator, the box said. Fits one six-pack, the box said. Convenient handle. Fits just right at desks, no more sharing with co-workers and putting your leftovers at risk. It was glossy and new, like the ones in the appliance department at Sears. Only *miniaturized*. She thought of the uncle, who wasn't even her real uncle; he'd been married to her mother's sister—he was fusty, never listened. Even though her mother had died, sometimes he'd appear out of the transom as though nothing had changed. She pictured her father in the house in the suburbs, grinding his teeth while holding the cordless telephone, listening to him talk. Right, her father would say. I see.

Someone bumped her elbow trying to get to their post office box, inserting the key, opening that little door. The fridge: obviously a regift. Presented to him by some colleague in the Department of Political Science at last year's Christmas party. She winched it out of the box, stuffed all the ridiculous packaging into the trash can. Out fluttered a note, an ecru envelope with her name written in immaculate handwriting. Was that her uncle's handwriting? She slid the note into her coat pocket and left for the office, exiting onto the noisy street, carrying the fridge by its handle.

I shall chalk this up to a good day, Audrey said.

❖ ❖ ❖

But: the twig. In addition to the refrigerator, there was the twig to consider.

She kept the twig in her right-hand pocket, touched it with her fingers. It was shaped like a Y, like a divining rod, a wishbone. The twig was worn soft from her touch. She liked to imagine it became softer each time she ran her fingers across it, until one day she would have held it long enough that it would in fact *become* a divining rod, and she would be able to find water beneath the concrete.

But the refrigerator. The *personal* refrigerator. It had a *handle*. It was substantial and rectangular, and so smooth and dustless. At the office, she unwound the cord from the convenient slot and slid the silvery prongs into the electrical outlet. A serene humming rose up. Its door made a satisfying bump when it closed. Now she could get to work. She sat at her desk with her strangely colored coat on. It was there humming when messages appeared in her inbox. Email was about to go down! Please use the fax machine instead.

While she tried to write the weekly status report, listening to people talking in the hallway, about this TV show, that boyfriend, it was humming. What did all these people have to talk about? Hey Audrey, Jameel said, you wanna try some of this candy I brought from Thailand? Hmm, she said, and she declined by saying actually she didn't much care for candy and really what she would like was a cigarette. Jameel laughed, thinking it was a joke. I'm emailing you the status report, she said, and she could feel that he wanted to be done with his status report but wasn't, and a shimmer of envy landed over all the filing cabinets.

In the evening she carried it to the grocery store, to see if things would fit inside it. Frozen peas, definitely. Box of cereal, unfortunately, no. At home in her apartment, with the piles of papers and other items all around, she set it on the counter, stretched the cord to the same socket where the regular refrigerator lived, and ate a bowl of cereal, and it sat there, humming. She smoked one cigarette out the window, and decided to give it a rest and unplugged it.

She went to sleep wearing the coat. The coat was the color of Dijon mustard. It was a color that often changed, she thought, depending on the light. American cheese. Tea with milk. Or perhaps not Dijon mustard but some other kind of mustard of the spicy German variety. As she lay in bed she listened to the traffic on the street below and told herself that the door had been locked, that she did not need to get up, and that when she woke she would still be wearing the coat, and perhaps it would be yet another color, which she could check in the morning in the new, different light. It was the best thing, how the light changed. How, the next day, there'd be things to collate and organize, and then after a while she would try to *stop*, stop thinking of braided rugs, stacked dishes, cans of pencils, people walking, a beach full of seashells, some French words, *toute soule*, round glasses, the sound of the radio announcer's voice, and the coat's yellows, and she would say to herself, shh, shh.

Pretty much all the time, Audrey had a lot of things to think about.

And slowly, as a few days passed, the fridge entered her consciousness as a *thing*. After that first day, she decided she would take it with her for a few more days, to see if it would be *useful*, she thought. One evening, when she held the twig in her pocket, walking home past the dry cleaner and the tire shop, it seemed so unclean and small. So, she placed it in the spot in her apartment that all *things* go, in a plastic bin under the bed. Inside was a very small fork. A tape measure slash keychain. A bag of peanuts. A pen from the Conrad hotel, that had been mercilessly twirled between two fingers of her right hand until her wrist ached.

And so it was that the age of the twig came to an end, and the era of the refrigerator began.

At this very moment it seemed, Audrey received another important message in the mail: Jury Duty. It was Wednesday, after work, and she stood in her apartment, taking off her coat. The notice was a complicated envelope with instructions for opening it. JURY SUMMONS, it screamed. She opened it, creasing, tearing, until it was a delicate thing, a sheaf of cards dangling by perforations.

Okay, she said. Okay.

For a while she stood in the bedroom, while whoever lived upstairs ran on the treadmill they kept in their apartment. She listened to the humming, the thumping, thinking about whether or not to put the coat back on.

❖ ❖ ❖

The morning of jury duty there was the kind of weather that wanted to destroy you, the kind that improved the indoors. It was snowing. She thought, perhaps I will leave the fridge here today. As she walked out the door, she saw it on the counter, looking lonesome, needing to be plugged in. At the last second, she grabbed it, and together, they were off.

She went to the courthouse and they said, Wrong courthouse, you want the green courthouse. When she found the place it was an auditorium full of people waiting, sitting in chairs. They were looking at Blackberries and reading newspapers and working on SuDoKu and as she sat down she thought how much the fridge looked like a white briefcase. A man talking into a microphone from a podium directed them to watch a video featuring Ed Bradley and Diane Sawyer and some councilperson who said, See? You are very important to the system but the system is very important to you.

Around the auditorium were stragglers, arriving late, wandering, scanning the room for seats. Audrey saw a man near her in the aisle. He was not tall, possibly near her age, she thought. He was handsome; he had a long forehead, and for a moment she caught herself staring, thinking, what must it be like to have a face like that, to shave every day, and she thought of shaving brushes, of him brushing his hair out of his eyes. She could feel him standing near and tried not to look up, but then she was filled with a curiosity, like staring into a crowded nightclub from a cold sidewalk. She looked and he was leaning down, his eyes blue, a kind of cerulean. He said, Pardon me? She was certain she saw something shift in his gaze, saw the line between his eyes soften, and he stepped past to sit in the seat next to her. He was skinny and covered with snow, fashionable in a disheveled way. He scooted in the chair, the snow dripped off his jacket. He sniffed, and she wished he would leave. She wondered where she could plug in the fridge. Perhaps not so much cerulean as *royal* blue. Would it be possible for someone's eyes to shift depending on the light? She wanted to look again.

The fridge was sitting there, cold, not humming, not in the slightest.

The man up front read some rules. DO NOT EAT IN THE JURY ROOM. DO NOT TALK ON YOUR CELL PHONE. DO NOT TAMPER WITH THE INTERNET ACCESS TERMINALS, THERE ARE SECURITY CAMERAS. DO NOT ASK ME TO REPEAT YOUR NAME. THERE IS ANOTHER PERSON THROUGH THESE DOORS TO YOUR LEFT MY RIGHT WHO WILL REPEAT YOUR NAME. AFTER WE COMPLETE THIS PROCESS I WILL TURN ON THE CNN FOR YOUR COURTESY.

He read some other rules allowing various classes of people to be excused, saying, finally, IF YOU DO NOT SPEAK ENGLISH WELL ENOUGH TO UNDERSTAND A TRIAL, PLEASE EXIT THORUGH THE DOORS TO MY LEFT.

Most of the room stood up to leave. The man said, OH, NOW YOU UNDERSTAND ENGLISH?

When the announcements were over, she waited, watching people get up and get coffee from a vending machine or use the pay phones in another room. She pulled the fat novel out of her bag and began to read.

Finally, her name was called amid a stack of names.

There it was. The halting, mashing of invented syllables that occurred when people attempted to read her impossibly long surname.

She followed the others who had been called to another room. You've been chosen for jury selection! said a guard with a ring of keys the size of a discus jangling from his belt. We'll be going upstairs, for a criminal trial.

The guard took them to a gleaming blonde-wood courtroom with a graying lady judge sitting at the bench, and a squad of attorneys at the tables, staring over their shoulders at them as they filed in. The guard announced that everyone should move in, and they squeezed together in the seats, which were like pews, coats crinkling together.

The fashionable guy was again seated next to her. How had she not noticed? He took off his coat, and underneath he seemed slight. His wrists were covered in bracelets that made him seem somehow tough, despite their being shimmery, colorful. Ahead of her was a man with a bald shining head, a plastic bag on his lap containing what appeared to be a box of donuts. Audrey set the fridge between her ankles, which didn't quite leave enough room for the guy, whose stomach was growling.

Sorry, he said to her. I'm really hungry, sorry.

Audrey looked down at the fridge. There wasn't anything to eat in the fridge. Could this be what he was asking? It occurred to Audrey that he was being chatty, that that's what people did. They made comments.

There's nothing to eat here, it would seem, she said.

Someone sneezed, and he said, Bless you. The judge said that the attorneys would ask them some questions, and then repeated a line from the Diane Sawyer film about listening with an open mind.

An open mind, Audrey thought.

You can't say, I *think* I can listen with an open mind, said the judge. You either *can*, or you can't.

They were led out again through a maze of brightly lit hallways. One at a time they were led back into the courtroom, only on the other side, no longer spectators, and filed into the jury box. She felt as though she was under a spotlight, and that no room had ever been brighter in the entire world. The guard read a statement. The defendant was being accused of robbery with a loaded gun. The defense attorney and the defendant looked strikingly similar, with their twin shining heads, their twin suits. The attorneys took turns asking questions to the prospective jurors.

Do you have a bias toward cops?

Do you feel you can put your feelings towards guns aside?

What if there is no physical evidence? How would you feel about *that*?

Audrey thought, I cannot answer these questions. I will have no answer. And what about the office? I cannot sit on this jury. She thought of stacks of papers in letter trays at her desk.

The answers that came out of the mouths of the others in the jury box were like tiny manifestos. I believe everything that a priest says! I believe in property rights! My son has a cleft palette!

The defense attorney stood over them with a pen in hand and a stack of rumpled papers and said, Miss—uh—Miss, uh, Audrey?

Yes? she said.

Can you?

Can I what?

Could you answer the question?

Could you repeat my name?

The defense attorney looked confused.

Audrey, he said.

I mean, could you repeat the *question*. I did hear that we were told *not* to ask for our names repeated, and I apologize. I meant to ask for the *question* to be repeated. That's what I meant. The *question*.

There was a long pause.

Certainly, the attorney said. Can you rely solely upon testimony of the victim to convict someone?

I can say that I have never thought about that at all, not at all. Pretty much never thought about that, she said.

Okay, he said, and made a mark on the legal pad in front of him.

When it was over, everyone filed out again, and sat in the pews while the attorneys conferred at the bench, the judge holding her hand over the microphone.

They ain't pickin me, a man said, sitting in the front row, They ain't pickin me. I ain't voted in ten years. Not since REAGAN.

The lawyers at the front of the bench dispersed, breaking like a football team from a huddle, and the bailiff returned and read a list of names.

There was hers.

She was juror number ten.

Oh thank god, a woman nearby said, obviously set free, grabbing her temples.

Wait! Audrey thought. The other people seemed to be looking around warily, peering to see who had been chosen. I have to write status reports! Audrey thought. But it occurred to her that this wasn't true, that Jameel would write his vastly inferior status report and read a glossy RSS feed and eat a chocolate bar and lick the wrapper, and her desk would stay empty. Many days she invented a task: stapling, for example. That satisfying noise, that controlled destruction. And she thought, no, she did not have to send out status reports.

Those of you not selected, you can go home now, said the judge, And we are very sorry. Those of you on the jury, you can come back tomorrow at 9:30. SHARP!

Then someone's cell phone rang.

There are no cell phones! said the judge.

❖ ❖ ❖

As Audrey made her way home she felt a sense that she had accidentally uttered a terrible secret. She went to the shop, not the grocery store but the smaller one with the Lithuanian flags in the window, the spotless shelves, the nice Lithuanian brothers working behind the counter, and no one, not ever, shopping. How are you, pretty? said one of the brothers. He was straightening the napkins on the counter.

I'm good! she said, and made a gesture like a little wave.

She went through the narrow, empty aisles, and leaned her head as near as she could to the things on the shelves, closing one eye—how straight they were, like a suspension bridge. In a whirl she picked up a basket and took some things: new dish sponge! Dryer sheets! Parsley! She paid at the front; the kind brother whisked the things into a bag and said, Good night! And as she walked home she felt free, that erroneous feeling gone, and she thought of herself with someone else, a man, the two of them walking to a restaurant, laughing as they ate, him following her up the stairs to her apartment, shaking the snow off his jacket, running down to pick up something they'd forgotten, and the two of them neatly stacking the new items in the cabinet, and later going to sleep in pajamas. But as she reached the steps of her apartment, she was alone, the picture dissolved, a lone sheet of newspaper under her feet.

Stop it, she said to herself. Just stop it.

Inside, she tried to do the things she always did. She turned on the radio. She made a bowl of cereal. She took all the glasses out of the cabinet, washed the shelf, put them back.

After a while she took out the box of *things*. She laid them out, until they covered the carpet. She found a dried napkin with scrawled words in many hands, stick figures, tic tac toe, the ink running. An arrow. The word *drunk*. *Hey!* it read. *What's up, biotch*, it read. Had she had drinks in a bar? With people who'd written on a napkin? It seemed apparent that she had. But she couldn't remember, not at all.

She left the things out, saw the bag from the shop on the counter. It hadn't been put away. She took off the coat at last.

Then, something fell from its pocket. The gift card from the fridge. How had she missed it? She stared at it in shock, the erroneous feeling returning with a crash. She must have known it was there, but never opened it. She read it:

Dear Audrey, this is a sadly belated present. Your mother and Lydia bought this when your mother was visiting us. I could never get it to the post office. One day I found it in the trunk of my car and thought I would wrap it up and send it to you as a birthday present. When they bought it, I seem to recall your mother making a comment that it looked like a toy, like one you had when you were small. I think your mother would have wanted you to have it.

Audrey sat at the table. The fridge hummed. But was it for *me?* she thought. Did they buy it for *me?* Audrey thought of her mother, eight inches shorter than her father. Her mother polishing the legs of the dining room table. The drawer full of pens in the end table. Pens. The first time she had met a thing, it had been a pen, or rather three pens in a packet, pearlescent blue plastic with a silver button to retract the point. Given to her by the receptionist in a psychologist's office, where she'd sat in elementary school, her father saying, Audrey, get up from there and get over here. Those are for you, the psychologist lady had said, they're yours. See? her mother said. Say thank you. When they'd run out of ink she saved them like shells collected from a beach, snails long dead and gone. Then there'd been the science fiction novels, the same in a series. The slinkys in a shoebox. And

the business cards, snatched from every place she went, stacked and wrapped with rubber bands. Her father saw her collect one of the dusty cards at Corby's Dry Cleaner. When they got home, he hung up his starched shirts and hissed, What are you *doing* with these, and took them all, in their little bundles, to the trash with the lawn clippings. She thought of her mother, living the end of her life in an apartment complex with dumpsters near the entrance, not living with her father in that house full of carpet and dust. She thought of her mother, in a lobby, watching her father grow red-faced at an incompetent hotel clerk, her saying, it's okay, we can wait. Really!

A thought inflated in her mind. How could you leave me with him. How could you wish you were somewhere else. She looked at the fridge: When she bought you, she asked it, were you meant for me? Did you come all this way for me? Or do you wish you were somewhere else?

And she became lost, as though staring into the horrible patterned carpet of an old hotel room. She went to the bathroom and saw her face in the mirror. She opened the medicine cabinet.

She opened it again.

❖ ❖ ❖

The next morning she made her way back to the courtroom, where she stood in a crowd with the rest of the jurors near the elevators, until the guard led them through the labyrinthine hallways—hamster mazes, more or less—in a haze of rustling coats and sniffles, and they were sent to sit in a room, this yet more brightly lit than the courtroom, cramped, with a conference table and a bathroom. She sat in one of the cushy swiveling chairs, the fridge on her lap, looking for a plug. There was no plug that she could see. She saw the blue-eyed guy. He'd made it through to the other side. The people were all talking to each other and groaning and complaining about still having to be there. One woman had a copy of *O*, the Oprah magazine, and offered it to another woman, who wore a velour track suit. Thanks, I haven't read this issue yet and my daughter took my copy, the woman said. The man with the donuts from yesterday had yet more boxes of donuts, and had a booming voice. Oh my god, yo, he said. He stood up and set the bags on the table and distributed the boxes, which contained not donuts, but beef patties.

My brother owns a Golden Krust, he said.

Someone said, I was getting hungry.

I was really dying, man, said the blue-eyed guy. Thank you.

Damien, he said to the air. Then he pushed the beef patties in Audrey's direction.

She stared at the box. A man on her right said, Want any? She shook her head, and he reached over and pulled the box away. Mmm, still warm, he said. She held the fridge on her lap and looked at all of them casually talking. They became not creatures that could be stepped around and avoided, but people with names and particular sounds to their laughs and their chewing. She had to get the book from her bag. She leaned down, hunching over the fridge and retrieved the thick book, flipped to her bookmark. Somehow in all the rustling the room became silent and the only rustling was her rustling.

What are you reading? Damien said to her.

Nothing, she said.

You like fantasy novels?

No, she said.

That looks like it's a fantasy novel, he said.

It's not, she said.

I think I've heard of that series.

This isn't in any series.

I thought it was! Isn't that *Towers of Nightsong*?

No, she said.

So what is it, then?

It's just a book I'm reading. I'm what they call a big reader.

She looked at the page and the words seemed like a brick. He was staring at her but she could not look up.

What's that you have there on your lap? he asked.

It's a refrigerator, she said.

Oh, he said. Cool. What's inside? You got some beer in there?

No. Just stuff.

What stuff?

Nothing. Stuff.

Now the beef patty guy was listening. What do you have a little fridge for? he said.

I thought it would make things more interesting, Audrey said.

What? he said.

Nothing. I just have it.

Audrey's face began to burn.

Okay, Damien said. She glanced at him and his hands were lifted, as though backing away. I was just asking, he said.

They all chewed the beef patties. Someone mumbled something, and she could tell it was this again, this familiar sequence of events, that she knew from the playground, and birthday parties, and from people working behind counters at coffee shops, and staff meetings. Little comments under their breath. Here it came. She heard Damien say something in a quiet voice. They snickered.

So what else do you like to do in your spare time? Damien said, shouting down the table.

Leave her alone, said a woman who was reading what looked like a science textbook.

I bet I know what you like to do, he said. Do you sing into your hairbrush? Do you send videotapes to *American Idol*? Maybe roleplaying games? he said. How about washing your hair?

Audrey had one hand on the smooth, white finish of the fridge. For a moment the room opened up and she could see light coming in from the window, a cloud sliding across the sun, the rain about to stop, and she was looking down at herself being insulted, and she thought, Wow, and for a second it didn't matter what she said, because she would never see these people again, not in the coffee shop, not in a staff meeting, not ever. She turned and looked at him. He seemed to be about to burst with laughter.

I've never watched *American Idol*. And I think I wash my hair about as often as you do.

The entire room snickered and the woman with the textbook laughed out loud. Audrey thought how she really needed to plug in the fridge. The man eating a beef patty chuckled so hard that he began to cough. Audrey looked at Damien and somehow she was sure that his face had changed, and she tried to look, to see if maybe it had changed and it wasn't as lovely as it had been before, but he sat, looking down, no longer about to laugh.

A long silence fell around the room. Audrey tried to ignore it but couldn't. Or maybe it wasn't a silence. Maybe it was a silence that only she heard. She looked out the window. She thought, maybe now I can just make a gesture like a little wave and everyone will know I'm saying good-bye. She stood and looked for a plug, found one near the bathroom, plugged in the fridge.

Nothing happened. The fridge did not switch on. There was no humming. A ripple ran down Audrey's limbs.

Just then the guard came in. He said, Okay, everyone needs to line up now.

Audrey yanked the cord and got in line with everyone else, holding the fridge by its handle, everyone shuffling, adjusting, sneakers squeaking on the linoleum. The guard walked by and counted each person. He came to her.

What's that, ma'am.

Audrey felt her chest tighten.

It's a refrigerator.

A little whiff of crazy passed over the guard's face, a look she recognized for the first time right then, and he moved from foot to foot, keys ringing slightly.

You can leave your things over here. You don't need them in the jury box.

Audrey stood, squeezing the fridge's handle. She looked at the guard's keys, their ring pulling on his belt.

It has some things inside that I need, she said.

Is that like some kind of a medical thing?

Um, she said. I mean, no.

The line shuffled. From one corner of her eye she saw Damien step out of line, and then he was standing beside her. Let me hold that for you, he said.

No.

It's okay, he said.

No, I have it right here, it's fine, she said.

I'll hold it for you.

The shuffling in the hall came to a halt.

No, she said, and her eyes began to well.

Listen, Damien said. I'm sorry.

He came closer. From his wrist, off his lithe, fashionable body, he removed a bracelet from the myriad baubles, made of string, or very thin rope, tinkling charms hanging from it. Then he took her arm. His hands were soft, as though it was only cloth brushing her skin. She felt herself breathe in sharply as he slipped the bracelet around her wrist. From her other hand he took the refrigerator.

The door swung open. Jurors entering, said the guard. There was no time to see where he had taken the fridge; he had disappeared to the back of the line; they were filing into the courtroom and she could only see the man ahead of her, his pants swiping each chair as he shuffled forward. They were seated in the chairs and the light shone in her eyes.

The defense attorney continued with his instructions.

The next question is, could you convict based on the testimony of just one man?

If that testimony were credible and true?

If he were a reliable person?

Could you believe in the story of just one man?

I'll ask you, he said. I'll ask you, she said. Miss—

As she listened to the questions Audrey felt her feet rise from the ground. Now the questions were over. The attorney was about to say her name. There were thirteen faces looking. She looked down for the small, cold thing that had always been there. But it was not there. Instead—what was that?—around her wrist was a string of beads that to Audrey seemed as wide and bright as a crown.

She was about to answer.

They were all waiting.

Well, could she?

❖ ❖ ❖

Marilyn Joy

How We Come to Know

The sheer white curtain
billows from behind
as the wind's invisibility
comes into form through
the fabric's suppleness—
its slight permeability,
allowing just that trace of
ether to seep the intimate
weave of threads,
to push past the weft of
interlacing fibers and under
the soft pleated edges.

Some things are like that,
invisible until
they alter the shape of
the world around them, like
the breath—how it shifts
inside the chest and belly,
inviting a measured rise and
fall of life to be seen.
And a spoken word, subtle
at times, yet it can shape
the whole of your day with
what rests inside.

Brook J. Sadler

Everything is what it is

and not another thing.

Tonight the rain—
a drear refrain—
makes dark the little theater
of mind that is my ark.

A wind in the trees
sounds of applause,
and fast fill the gullies,
fast fill the ditches dug of doubt
before the storm blows out.

Morning's curtain rises—
sunlight spills its apricot nectar over the fields—
enter songbirds that never once rehearsed
their dew-winged and flitting play.
But I again, again must stage my claim
on sweet today.

* *"Everything is what it is and not another thing."*
    –Bishop Joseph Butler (1692-1752)

Disembark

Return home through a side door, into the kitchen
where a dish towel and absolute stillness
hang waiting, and the last-used glass
stands dry in the rack.

Arrive in time
to see an hour of daylight
trapped between the pressed
lips of the mini blinds.

In the refrigerator find
more than expected: two beers
standing tough among the condiments.
Hold one by the neck and twist. Toss
the cap on the counter. A cool offer
lisps from the bottle-mouth.

At the table, sit, now home
from another trip, and pause to consider
what has just begun: this re-inhabiting
of a life, the climb

back inside this scaffold of furniture and art.
Built on a few career-quality planks
nailed through with numbers and accounts.
Electric bulbs will invite
bills to swoop against the glass,
appointments to smack
each bright calendar pane
already sticky with tasks.

For now, leave all switches
untouched, heads bowed.
Remain seated and wait
for the dark. Feet propped
on a suitcase full of shirts
in need of washing.

Take another swig, a loose
mouthful of light in a room.

Katherine E. Young

If There Is a Hell

it resembles this street in shadow, this street
and this streetlamp, where you and I cling

so tightly our flesh bruises for weeks and
our mouths ache with the work of longing

it blinks cold, disapproving, like stars glimpsed
from hard ground as muscle grinds into grit

it feels, like your fingers, for tears on my cheek

it tastes of tea brewed by your wife, shakes
like her hand as she pours a cup for me

it kisses like my husband scenting you
on my lips, hunches his shoulders as if he might care

it cries like my son at my step on the stair,
as he finds he's stayed awake, after all

Carlos Almaraz, *Night Magic (Blue Jester)*, 1988, oil, Smithsonian American Art Museum, Gift of Gloria Werner. © 1988, Carlos Almaraz Estate. Reproduced courtesy of Museum of Fine Arts, St. Petersburg, from "Our America: The Latino Presence in American Art."

Kate Kaplan

Why We Like Vampire Movies

This is a second marriage for both of us, so when Amy and I got together it made sense for her to hold onto her house. She found a decent tenant, and it worked out ok for a few years. Then the tenant moved on, and real estate agents started telling her that the neighborhood had gotten so hot that it was time to cash out. Late last year, Amy put the house on the market, and it went fast, to an actor, a kid named Jasper who could afford to buy near the Hollywood sign because he'd played a vampire in a big movie.

Amy and I looked him up when the offer came in. According to the magazines, Jasper was really talented, and handsome in the way that counts these days—delicate but masculine, they said, or they said, exotic good looks.

I don't know what any of that means—he looked a little feminine to me—but Amy said that everyone, male and female, from the brokers to the chimney inspector, had crushes on Jasper. Amy might have had a crush on him herself, though she'd never have admitted it. All she said was that he was a nice kid who was trying to enjoy his success without turning into an asshole. That's an occupational hazard in Hollywood, as anyone who lives in this city knows.

At any rate, she was right about Jasper being a nice kid. He proved it by inviting us to his housewarming party.

Amy reminded me about it a couple of days in advance. We were having dinner, a barley and vegetable thing she'd picked up at Whole Foods. "We don't have to stay long," she said.

"It sounds like fun." That was an exaggeration. I'm a doctor, an orthopedic surgeon, and Tuesdays and Thursdays are my O.R. days. On a Saturday night, I'm as far as I get from making my incisions, staring at my monitor, and inserting my instruments into somebody's knee. Saturday nights, I like to drink a little wine, and, weather permitting, sit out on the deck.

You can see the whole San Fernando Valley from my deck. During the day the view is of streets and houses, and I like that, but at night it's really something special; bright lights from the streets and dim lights from the houses, and patches of dark on the hillside that make all the lights look brighter, just the way an artist might paint it. Even the freeways look great, streams of red and white that go on and on, everyone headed somewhere, no matter what the hour.

But going to Jasper's party seemed like the right thing for a husband to do. "I want to go," I said. "Say goodbye to the place."

Amy nodded. "That's what I thought. Out with the old. In with the new." But she looked sad. I thought, not for the first time, that her decision to sell had something to do with the fact that her daughter had decided to go to college on the east coast. Becca had only been gone a year, and we both missed her.

"There are a lot of memories in that house," I said.

"Memories," Amy said dismissively. "You get to keep those." She poured herself another half-glass of Pinot Noir. "I just think it'll be good to have a break from the usual Amy-and-Dan routine."

For a surgeon, routine isn't a problem, it's a goal. We do things the same way every time, and even if there's something unexpected, it isn't really unexpected. If we're any good—and we are, in my practice—we've anticipated it and we have a protocol. Hell, I've kept my shirts and socks organized in exactly the same way since med school. That's how much I like predictability.

But operating room rules don't always make sense outside the O.R. I learned that late—too late—in my first marriage. I tried again. "Talk about repeating yourself. Tomorrow I'm repairing an ACL I repaired eight years ago. Re-tear." Actually, it's an interesting surgery, and if older people—people like me—keep playing sports, I'll be doing more of it.

"You could switch specialties," Amy said, although she knows I can't. She has that characteristic, that's supposed to be a male characteristic, where she tries to find a solution every time she hears about a problem, or thinks she does. That's great at her job—she's the HR manager at a big engineering firm—and it usually worked with our kids—Becca and my two boys, when the boys were with us—but I sometimes find it hard to take.

I forked up a chunk of sweet potato. "I yam what I yam."

Amy liked that. She gave me her best smile, the one where her whole pretty face is full of pleasure. "Really?" she teased. "What about the transformative power of spinach?"

"Not substantiated by the scientific literature. And not a cure for thyroid orbitopathy."

"Pop eyes are thyroid?"

"Right. He probably needed steroids."

"Poor old Popeye," Amy said. "Poor old guy."

❖ ❖ ❖

I was ready for bed before Amy was, which is common. I have early surgeries and patient appointments, and she's a night owl. Usually, she's reading or working or on the phone with Becca, who's a night owl herself. That night, she was in front of the TV, a cooking show on the screen and the remote in her hand.

"What's on?" I asked, prepared to stay up a little later than I should, to be with her.

"Not much." She switched to a movie; children screaming with joy on a roller coaster.

"That roller coaster's doomed," I said.

"Doomed," Amy agreed, her eyes still on the screen. Then she lowered the sound. "You know what it's going to be? Jasper's party?" She answered her own question. "It's going to be a party full of young people, where we're no one's parents. How long since we did that?"

"We're not that old," I said. I'm sixty, and Amy's almost ten years younger, but the fact was that we'd never been to a party full of young people where we were no one's parents, because we hadn't been young together.

"Not that young, either," Amy said, and I said, "Hey!"

She gave me a smile and reached over to pat my hand, but it didn't seem like she wanted company. "Don't stay up too late."

"I won't," Amy said, but she did.

❖ ❖ ❖

My practice is managed by an extremely competent administrator, but my partners and I have agreed that one of us must be involved in any major decision. It's a good rule, and we take turns, but it meant that I spent most of the next day talking to software vendors.

The only patient I saw was a guy I had to turn down for surgery, something I like even less than I like dealing with the business end of the practice. People think that all us orthopods are in that specialty because we're jocks, or former jocks, but that's not the whole story. I like ortho because the work's steady and lucrative. I like it because the knee is something you can master, and it's a great feeling, being totally on top of something. I like it because I can almost always help the patient. Not this time. The MRI indicated that surgery was necessary. His pain level did too, but I couldn't cut as long as he was taking Coumadin, and his cardiologist predicted terrible things if he stopped. The guy was going to have to suffer, and there was nothing I could do.

❖ ❖ ❖

The day left me feeling restless and tight. When I got home, I decided to go for a run. If anyone knows what running does to your knees, it's me. Switch to a brisk walk, I tell my patients. Swim. Use an elliptical. It's the advice I've given myself, and unlike my patients, I'm mostly compliant.

That day, though, the pool or the elliptical machine wasn't going to do it. I didn't want the privacy of my back yard, and I didn't want to watch the news or listen to a podcast, which is the only way I can get through a session on the elliptical. I wanted to be outside. I wanted the small danger of tripping over a tree root or broken bottle, so that I had to be alert. I wanted to move.

❖ ❖ ❖

I drove down to the park—it used to be in running distance, but it isn't anymore—and ran on the path. I wasn't a particularly fast runner when I ran every day, and I'm certainly not now. That doesn't matter. Even slow, the run felt great. I'm not talking about runner's high, some big rush of endorphins, though I have felt that.

It's this: my route took me past a leaky sprinkler head, and every time I passed it, I saw a crow at the little puddle. The crow had a big piece of what looked like hot dog bun, and the first time I saw him, I thought he'd accidentally dropped the bun into the puddle. Lost his dinner, I thought, but on my next lap, I saw him do it again, and then I understood. He was dropping the bun into the puddle on purpose, getting it soft enough to eat. For a few more laps that smart old crow, fixing his dinner, fully occupied my head. No room for anything else. And in a few more laps even the crow was gone, and all that was happening was motion, and that's bliss.

One of my colleagues, an ankle guy, says that humans were made for running or walking, for on-foot locomotion, and that no one can be deeply happy without it. Logically, it's an overstatement, but that day it seemed to me that he was dead right.

❖ ❖ ❖

Amy was there when I got home, still in her work clothes, but with her shoes off, making a salad for dinner. She knew right away where I'd been. "Danny!" she said. "Sweetheart! Love of my life! You'll be sore for a week." She opened the freezer and reached for an ice pack.

"I drove down," I said defensively, gulping a glass of water. Unfortunately, my back chose that moment to spasm, and I couldn't hide it, because it hurt enough that I had to stretch. I got down on the floor, knees bent and feet flat, and pulled one knee into my chest. "Count of twenty. I'll be fine."

"Oh, Danny," Amy said, and I said, "I don't do it very often."

"I know, just, don't go for the mid-life crisis, ok? No sports car." She said it lightly, but with an edge.

I'd loved driving sports cars. It wasn't about the speed, though I'd liked that, back when you could get enough open road in L.A. to drive fast. It was the engineering, the handling, the connection to the car and the road. I had a beautiful little vintage XKE for a while. Way too showy and not very reliable, but man was it great to drive. Great then, but my reflexes have slowed. Now I have a car with an automatic transmission. It's small like a sports car, but it isn't one.

I stood up and gave Amy a kiss, careful not to rub my sweaty t-shirt against her nice blouse. "Sweetheart, I'll buy a Volvo wagon if that's what you want. I swear, no crisis of any kind."

I meant it. When you have everything you want, it's not good to want something else.

❖ ❖ ❖

Saturday, I had a partner's meeting and Amy went shopping for something to wear to Jasper's party.

Saturday night, when I went into the bedroom to change into a clean shirt, I found Amy standing in her closet wearing something I'd never seen before, black pants and a long-sleeved black top that fit close to her body and sparkled at the neck. She looked terrific. She almost always does, though I admit that I like to see her wearing skirts more than she likes wearing skirts. She has great legs.

She was staring at a pair of shoes—black high heels—and she looked unhappy.

"The shoes are nice," I offered.

"The shoes are fine." For a minute, I didn't think she was going to say anything else, but she did. "I keep thinking, what would I be wearing to this party if I were Jasper's age?"

"A flower behind your ear?"

She shrugged. "Something like that."

There is, or was, a yellow silk flower in her top dresser drawer, on a little comb so that it can be worn in your hair. Amy's hair. I saw it a couple of years ago when I was looking for a necklace she'd asked me to bring her—we were meeting downtown for dinner before the Philharmonic.

It's a little hard for a husband to think about, his wife before he knew her; Amy before even her first marriage, all the switches turned to On, showing off everything she had no matter how modestly she was dressed—and I wouldn't bet on that—ready to see who, or how many, she could charm. She would have been dazzling. She is now, but it's different.

"You look lovely," I said. "You are lovely."

Amy kissed my cheek. "Thanks. But you know, I have that incurable disease." Then she finished the old joke. "Being alive."

❖ ❖ ❖

How often had I made that drive, going to see Amy, going home from Amy's, going somewhere with Amy next to me in the car?

We both got quiet when I turned off Franklin and twisted up into Amy's old neighborhood, which is where silent movie stars lived in the twenties and where cowboy actors lived in the thirties, where nobody famous lived when Amy lived there and where everybody like Jasper wants to live now.

"Gloria Swanson house," I said, as we drove past an old Tudor. There's a rumor that Joe Kennedy'd once bought that house for Gloria Swanson, and that's what the ads say every time the house is for sale, that that's the rumor. No one bothers to figure out whether it's true, because no one cares. The rumor is a good enough provenance. Amy and I had always laughed about that.

"Gloria Swanson," Amy said. "Gloria Nobody. After tonight, I'll probably never see that house again." She opened the window, then shut it again, then fidgeted with an earring—the coral ones I'd given her for Christmas. Then she sighed. "Ok, I admit it. There's a little bit of road-not-taken. Not that I wanted to be an actor, but it's not like I spent my girlhood yearning to go into HR, either. Anything could have happened, and this is what did."

I parked the car uphill from Amy's old house. It was a difficult spot on a curving bit of street, but I'd figured it out when Amy and I were dating and I had it in muscle memory. I did it perfectly, and I liked that. "We happened," I said.

"Oh, Dan," Amy said. "Of course, and I'm so glad about that. It's just . . . you know."

I did, I think.

❖ ❖ ❖

That old thing about the prettiest girl and handsomest boy from every high school in America going to L.A.—at Jasper's house that night, it looked like that was true.

They were crowded into Amy's old living room and spilling out on to Amy's old balcony, talking and laughing and drinking beer from bottles and wine from plastic cups. Music was playing downstairs and the smell of marijuana was coming from the upstairs bathroom.

"I'm wearing enough fabric to dress six of these women," Amy whispered to me. An exaggeration, but not by much. The average female outfit was a tiny dress or something like a t-shirt, lace shorts, and what looked like fancy hiking boots. The average male was wearing jeans and a sweat-er, not that different from what I had on—as Amy points out, life's not fair that way.

"Goddamn but they're young," I said. "Wonder if they even know who Popeye is?" Amy looked at me blankly. "No great loss if they don't," she said, and then Jasper came up and gave her a hug and shook my hand.

"Still loving the house?" Amy asked him.

"Loving it!" he said. "Let me show you!"

❖ ❖ ❖

It was strange to see Amy's house decorated to someone else's taste. The house is partly Spanish style, which in L.A. means a red tile roof and archways between the rooms, but the builders had either forgotten about Spain by the time they got to the bedrooms, or else they couldn't afford it anymore. Amy used to say that it was a house that couldn't decide what it wanted to be when it grew up.

Amy's ex was unreliable when it came to child support, and when Amy lived in the house things were a little shabby; beat-up tile in the bathrooms and a kitchen that looked like the eighties remodel it was. Still, the place had personality. For instance, the kitchen cabinets were just paint-grade ply, but Amy and Becca painted the insides bright pink, so that when you went for a glass or a cup or whatever, you got a nice little shock, even if you knew it was there, from that burst of color. I liked that so much that I'd wanted to repeat it when Amy and I redid our kitchen, but Amy wanted glass-front cabinets and cool colors—her dream kitchen, she said, now that she had the chance.

Amy's pink cabinets were gone, along with the rest of the old kitchen. Jasper had put in dark wood and stone on the counters and fancy appliances he probably wouldn't use. He'd redone the bathrooms, too, and put down wood floors where Amy'd had carpet. The furniture wasn't all new, though. According to his decorator—one of the young women in shorts—a lot of it was from thrift shops or secondhand stores, and it wasn't because Jasper couldn't afford new. Old and used was the new fashion. Didn't matter. Everything still seemed new, because it was so clearly new to him.

❖ ❖ ❖

Amy's good at meeting people. Good at parties. I mostly hung out on the balcony, looking at Amy's city view. A couple of the kids said hello and asked me how I knew Jasper, and when I told them they said how much they liked the house and how great it was that Amy and I were at the party. After that, we didn't have much to say, but I was happy enough just to listen.

Apparently, Jasper was going to play a science professor in a new movie. "At least he won't have to hit the gym every damn day, like we did on *Signs*," one guy said. *Signs and Wonders* was Jasper's vampire movie. "I never did figure out why vampires take their shirts off so much."

"Vampires are show-offs," another young man said. "Well-known fact."

One of the women gave the first guy an affectionate shove. "The women of America appreciate those workouts. That's why we stare at you. Because we respect your hard work."

The guy just grinned and grinned.

❖ ❖ ❖

After a while, I went looking for Amy. I found her downstairs in what had been Becca's playroom. Now it had a big tv and a leather sofa, and a table made out of an old trunk, but all that was pushed up against a wall. There was music—I guess Motown never dies—people were dancing. Amy was one of them.

She was with some guy about Jasper's age, but they didn't look wrong together, just two people enjoying the same song—"Dancing in the Street," Martha and the Vandellas. Amy was graceful and the boy was klutzy, but they were both singing along.

Amy saw me just as the song ended and another began—"My Girl." Over the music, I heard her say, "Ok if I dance with my husband?" and I took Amy into my arms.

"That kid a good dancer?" I asked her.

"Nope." She glanced over at him. He wasn't leading, just leaning into the girl he was dancing with. "Young men know nothing, as all young women eventually learn."

"Good to know," I said, and pulled her closer.

Amy and I have always liked dancing together, but we hadn't done it in a long time—not since the last time we'd been to a wedding, probably. I thought it and Amy said it. "What's wrong with us, that we don't dance unless somebody gets married?"

"We're crazy," I agreed, enjoying the feel of her body against mine. I'm glad to say that I enjoy that pretty often, but it's different when you're dancing, and it's different when you're dancing in a room that used to be your step-daughter's playroom, that's full of young people singing along to music you've loved since you were as young as they are. It's wonderful, but it's disconcerting, too.

Someone yelled down the stairs. "Taco truck!"

"The fancy kind, right?" I asked Amy. "Not the construction-site kind?" Which I sometimes stop at, against my better judgment, when the temptation's too great.

"Very fancy," Amy said. "Kimchi quesadillas and all that."

The smell of grilled meat was starting to filter into the house, but I wanted to dance with Amy until the song ended. Really, I wanted to dance with her for much longer than that.

❖ ❖ ❖

A couple of Amy's old neighbors were outside near the taco truck. I'd never liked them, or anyway I'd never liked him. Ben pretends to be a thoughtful, caring guy, but actually, he's a horse's ass. I have no idea what his wife is like. Sarah never gets a word in.

Ben asked us the conventional questions, how we were and how Becca was doing, even how my sons are. When he heard that everyone was thriving, he turned contemplative. "Look at all this," he said, his glance taking in the house, the taco truck, the happy, good-looking kids. "What a sad comment on society! Teachers make nothing, but some twenty-five-year-old actor has all this." Ben wasn't a teacher; he owned a dry cleaner and he did pretty well, but that didn't stop him. "And for pretending to be a vampire, of all things. A lot of nonsense."

"I bet you didn't even see that movie," Amy said rudely, which surprised me. Ben didn't usually get under her skin the way he did mine.

"Sure I did," Ben said. "Sarah and I wanted to check out our new neighbor. I suppose it was entertaining, but beyond that . . . ." He shrugged. "A fairy tale."

"No it wasn't," Amy said. "In a fairy tale there's a reason for everything that happens to people. Even if it's a jealous fairy at someone's cradle, there's a reason. And a moral, too. There weren't any reasons in Jasper's movie, and no morals, either."

Ben raised his hands in mock surrender. "Ok, ok, it wasn't a fairy tale. My point is, big box office, thousands of people saw it, but it wasn't *about* anything."

"Was it?" I asked Amy—just Amy. I didn't care about Ben, but Amy was talking as though fairy tales and Jasper's movie really mattered to her. I had to know what she thought.

"Oh, Danny," she said, looking at me as if she wasn't sure I'd understand. "It was about mystery. It was weird and dark and the whole movie, nobody human understood what was going on. Forces unseen. That's what it was about. That's why we like vampire movies."

I reached for her hand, but she'd turned away. Jasper and the other guy from the movie were outside too, and they must have heard the conversation, because they'd drifted toward us. "What do you think?" Amy was asking Jasper. "Ben says that *Signs* wasn't about anything. I think he's wrong."

Jasper was such a nice kid that he gave Ben an earnest, respectful look. "Yeah," he said, "I get it, a movie's like a bunch of kids playing let's-pretend. But on *Signs*, we kind of took it seriously. I know it sounds like actor bullshit, but we thought the movie was about fear, and like Amy says, the stuff that goes on or that we like sense is going on, that we can't see, or understand at all."

"Right," Jasper's buddy chimed in. "It's vampires, and that's ridiculous, but everybody's got a vampire in them, or else they're afraid they do. That's how I played it, anyway."

"Dan!" Ben said. "Help me out! What do you see when you look inside people? Vampires?"

It did sound like actor bullshit. Jasper and his friend had glided through the short beginnings of their lives cushioned by luck and their good looks. They knew nothing—how could they? I thought that, but it wasn't everything I thought, and Amy was waiting for my answer. I smiled at Ben. "Can't help you. Mystery wouldn't show up on an arthroscope. It's not the right instrument."

That earned me one of Amy's lovely smiles, the one where her whole pretty face is full of pleasure. "Listen to the man," she said softly.

Jasper's pal handed me a Noche Buena, which is just the kind of dark Mexican beer I like, and

damn hard to find. He clinked his bottle against mine, then against Jasper's. "And how does mystery speak to us?" he asked Jasper. There was a church in that kid's background somewhere.

"Through signs and wonders," Jasper answered.

"Through vampire movies?" Ben asked snottily.

"Damn straight," Amy said. "Through vampire movies."

❖ ❖ ❖

Amy was quiet on the way home. "Ben's an ass," I said, when we were on the freeway, making our own contribution to that endless stream of light.

"He's probably right." She leaned her head on the window glass, something that always makes me nervous. "It was just a movie. A lot of good-looking kids, half-naked on the screen."

I told her what Jasper's buddy had said about vampires stripping down, and the way the young woman had reacted. That got a smile, but then a sigh. "Yeah, in Hollywood the vampires are all young and cute and in great shape. Which is a waste, because kids like that already think they're immortal." Unlike the rest of us. That went unsaid.

❖ ❖ ❖

I woke up just before dawn. Amy wasn't in bed and the light wasn't on in the bathroom, either. I found her on the deck, wrapped in the blanket we keep on the family room couch for cold nights. She was leaning on the rail and looking out into the Valley.

I was barefoot, in shorts and a t-shirt, but I went out anyway. "Come inside," I said, putting my hand on her shoulder. She did, I think mostly to get me out of the cold.

We didn't go back to bed, just sat on the couch and watched the day arrive on the other side of the sliding glass doors. After a while, I made coffee. We didn't talk much.

We have mysteries facing us, Amy and I, and if they're speaking through signs and wonders, well, I can't hear it. I know that what I see isn't all there is, but I don't know if I want to see the rest of it. Then again, I don't know that I have a choice. It's too late for us to be vampires. Not Hollywood vampires, anyway.

❖ ❖ ❖

Jenna Rindo

Ode to Bones—Compact and Spongy

"I am poured out like water, and all my bones are out of joint"
–Psalm 22:14

Bones hold the hopeful aura of their hosts,
house purity within their prominent processes,

their necessary depressions. They reflect light, though they are pocked
and battered by injuries in layers. Each bone contains the sticks and stones

of adolescent breakage. Haunted skulls almost smooth with
fused cranial sutures, gaping sockets once captured visions

in color. Jaws no longer grind against bad dreams or masticate meat.
The Body Worlds skeletons are a strange shade of cream, each

piece charted and named in Latin, housed in Plexiglas boxes.
Long bones fork like a rod to divine some

orthodox resting place. Her femur, cross-cut, exposing cavities
filled with marrow that brewed the broth of her

blood, once rich and rude with the stink of life. Her tarsal heel weary
held in metal stirrups, straining with birth, pelvic ligaments

loosened to allow the passage of newborn crowns. Her wrist ossified
porous, once bangled by a tarnished silver bracelet,

metacarpals tossed in the box like tangled charms. Flat bones
believe in eternity—they learn

by holding what they have to hold:
the heart, the bullet, the brain's intricate folds.

This Random Heart

. . . muscular, cone-shaped organ, about the size of a clenched fist

Our palms up, open to receive this random
heart, so severely severed from
its host, now released from its cage
of ribs, combed out of the meshed net of
pericardium, our Body Worlds Guide presses
it into our hands, demands we weigh it simultaneously.

Once vivid, oxygen-rich, a bifurcated
aorta racing with scarlet bliss, now the chemical
color of Silly Putty. It's a cliché
the size of my fist. Four chambers dipped
in some polymer patented *Plasticene*.
Unable to murmur secrets through the stethoscope's
diaphragm into her doctor's ear.

The guide can't narrate any biographical
details involving donors yet I dwell
in details. Was her heart amply stocked
with love? Did fear slosh up, backflow
her valves? Did her children make great
weighty demands? Did they eat her heart out?

My husband and I exchange glances. We're dumb
struck, unable to explain our own skipped beats for
first lust, the race up flights of orgasmic stairs.
Before I hand it back to our guide I want to bring
it to my face and smell some urgent stink
of heart break. I want to toss
this heart back and forth like a hot potato
then shake it to see if a tiny packet of desiccant
rattles inside like regret.

Bryce Berkowitz

Walk among Men
on State Street in Chicago

Whiskey burns scars that won't heal
In a past where a sodden man
Stands, back to the wall, outside Marshall Fields

Blowing his saxophone to pieces.
Then, the men with spikes bust concrete
In brown overalls, hard-headed, canary-yellow.

You hope the wind won't bruise your cheek.
You watch the white-knuckled security guard
Swat a bum for territory. You watch

The motorcade—the el train wheels sharpen blades.
The bridge snaps in half to lift her arms
Into the foggy twilight, so a river barge

Can fan the water. Sirens sing-a-long
To the rooftop balcony with your father.
Fireworks explode over the water and into the sky.

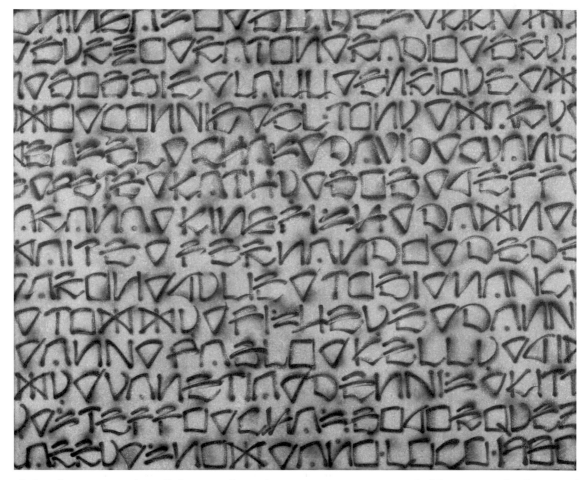

Charles "Chaz" Bojórquez, *Placa/Rollcall*, 1980, acrylic, Smithsonian American Art Museum, Gift of the artist. Reproduced courtesy of Museum of Fine Arts, St. Petersburg, from "Our America: The Latino Presence in American Art."

Rebecca Givens Rolland

We Don't Throw Sand:
Uncovering the Impulse Towards Others

It wasn't my finest parenting moment—that much was clear. My daughter Sophie was just under two, and we'd taken a long weekend trip to the North Carolina coastline to get away from the early snows and play on the beach. We'd taken our towels and plastic shovels out to the beach, and my husband Philippe had gone inside for his sunglasses. The day was a gorgeous one—brighter and sunnier than any in recent memory, with a direct light that made me squint.

We hadn't been to the beach in a while—the closest we'd gotten was a water table filled with toy boats on our common roof deck. Most recently, Sophie had played in the season's first snow, laughing and throwing loose snowballs in Philippe's and my face as she rolled around. We were grateful for the trip, grateful to get away at a time when the weather was sure to get worse.

Only a few minutes after we arrived, a girl a bit taller than Sophie sat down near us with a blond, freckled woman. With only a few others on the beach, we introduced ourselves—she was a high school English teacher who "needed a break." I nodded and watched as her daughter and Sophie began to play together, or rather argue over whose toy was whose. Coaxing each of them to trade a toy, we laughed at their half-successful, parent-induced attempts to "share."

The two of them were playing in silence, digging and scratching for shells in the sand, when all of a sudden, Sophie took a big handful of sand and threw it straight in her new friend's face. Her friend, without hesitation, started wailing and rubbing her eyes, crying that she had gotten sand in her eyes, that she couldn't see. I was alarmed, and the child's mother was too, holding her daughter tight, pleading with her to open her eyes, even a crack. Who knew if it was truth or melodrama—the point was, the girl was in pain,

and Sophie was the one who had caused it. Racing down the beach with Sophie trailing behind, I grabbed a bottle of water I'd left near my towel. "Here, take this," I offered. "Sorry. I'm so sorry." The girl's mother gave a half-nod and took it, tipping her daughter's chin up to rinse her eyes.

Sophie stared at her new friend—or non-friend, rather—blankly watching the scene unfold under the midday sun. Her face had the look of someone who'd only recently awoken from a dream. "She's hurt," I tried to explain to her, knowing it wasn't the worst thing that could have happened—she'd been around her share of biters—but upset and mystified, and frankly embarrassed, at how completely unprovoked it seemed. I'd rarely seen Sophie act angrily for no clear reason—and this time, she'd hardly even interacted with the girl before throwing sand.

I asked Sophie to apologize—one time, two—but she continued just to watch me, her face a puzzle, shaking her head. I ended up apologizing for her, I suppose because I felt I had to, that the injury was, by extension, my fault. The girl appeared to be fine in the end, and as we walked away, I wondered whether we'd heightened the drama by reacting so strongly.

Once it was just the two of us, I asked Sophie what had happened. It was her apparent lack of empathy I didn't understand, the fact that she sat and didn't react as the girl cried.

"I didn't know that sand hurt," she said, with a face in a sadder pout than I'd ever seen.

Suddenly it came to me—Sophie had spent much of her recent memory around water or snow, both of which she'd splashed about in happily, not worrying much if a bit spilled onto her parents or her friends. Only recently, we'd had a miniature snowball fight with the thin layer of snow on the ground. Her absence of empathy wasn't, I realized, a fundamental trait, but rather a misunderstanding about the way the world worked, a lack of knowledge about the differences between water and snow and sand.

"I see," I said to her, softening. "Now you know we don't throw sand." I let the matter go after that—in any case, there would be much bigger battles to be had—but it was Sophie who kept bringing the incident back. "Remember that girl?" she said to me at dinnertime night after night. "She got hurt. I hurt her."

"I know," I said to her. "But you're still learning. You didn't know."

"I didn't know," she said, reaching out for a hug. "We don't throw sand."

Her level of empathy was startling to me—rather than being careless, as I had initially thought, she in fact was worried deeply over whether that girl, whom she'd only met once, was all right. In the end, it was I who needed to help her get over the situation, I who needed to help her forget—or rather, to realize that we may hurt others without realizing it, that we need to apologize, but also that we can't let ourselves get too wound up over it. If we spent our lives worrying over past hurts, we'd never be able to engage with others freely— that certainly wasn't an outcome I wanted for her.

❖   ❖   ❖

Sophie's a few months past two now—she's traversing a literal growth spurt, and an explosion of language, which allows me much better insight into how she's thinking and feeling. In our Boston apartment, she hangs from the railing of her bed, gazing upward, as if she'd turn into an acrobat and fly from the ceiling if she could.

It's the depths of winter, when every hint of flower and shoot of leaf has gone underground— but she's flourishing like some camellia that can't be tamped down. Every day, I catch her speaking another new word, sometimes a phrase, with an increasingly nuanced tone of voice. All of a sudden, one day, she's "frustrated"—she repeats the word over and over, stomping her feet in the midst of her messy playroom like she must have seen someone do (not me, I assure myself). I ask her about it a couple times, then—once she repeats "I don't know why" twice—let it go, not sure that she knows what it means.

I've been reading books about emotions to her on purpose, driven in part by my doctoral research designed to expand children's and adults' emotional vocabulary. These books have characters who feel *joyous* and *disappointed, annoyed* and *hopeful* and *fabulous,* girls in bright polka-dot hats who climb trees and scale fences and fall. I don't expect that she'll understand or use all those words now, of course, but I'm interested in trying to expose her to that vocabulary early on, to let it soak into the background, to be used later on.

Sometimes she uses the words without clear awareness of what they mean—"I'm lonely," she'll say with a gleeful expression, flinging her arms around the room, or "I'm desperate." Sometimes she uses them for rhyming games she makes up, a tradition I started (cue the speech pathologist) but which she's taken to new heights of her own. "Lonely, bonely," she'll say. "That rhymes." Then: "Lonely, microwave. That doesn't rhyme! Your turn."

I laugh and let her use the words for fun. Later on, she'll get into what they mean—and I'll get to understand better how she's feeling, and hopefully allow her to better express herself.

If we can't identify and express what we are feeling, so the research goes, we're all the more likely to act out, or to turn those emotions in upon ourselves. *Emotional regulation* is the technical term—in learning to label our own emotions, we are better able to manage to express feelings in the ways we want and need. Whether it means managing one's own feelings of irritation when handling an argument between two children, or keeping feelings of disappointment about work, when needed, to oneself, emotional regulation is a key component of maintaining healthy emotional lives and helping ourselves and others to grow. The same is true for adults and for children—though children haven't learned the full range of emotional vocabulary, they often have a more direct link to their emotions than adults do.

Too often, we as adults have gotten good at hiding what we're feeling, either restricting our range of emotions to those that are acceptable— for instance, becoming uncomfortable with feeling or being the recipient of feelings of anger or feeling a range of emotions, but denying the fact that we do. In teaching Sophie about emotional language, I want to help her natural emotions come out, and help her grow up learning the nuances of her emotional life.

❖ ❖ ❖

As she continues growing, it is her strong sense of empathy that continues to surprise me, the same empathy I saw after the sand-throwing incident, but now stronger, and more nuanced, more refined. That sense of empathy—from the ancient Greek *empatheia*, originally meaning *suffering at or with*, translated into German as *Einfühlung*, or *feeling into*, only afterwards to arrive at our word—startles me in the way it is directed so strongly outward, at all kinds of creatures, but especially nonhuman ones.

These days, in big and small ways, Sophie starts showing us how she cares for dolls, for animals, for family, for plastic flamingoes that appear in the winter snow. "I love them," she says, patting them on their bright orange beaks, scaling them as though they're skyscrapers. Her "babies"—as there are many, ranging from an inch-long doll in her dollhouse to a pink stuffed dog to a plastic Lego man—all get houses of their own that she builds out of magnetic tiles. As she links one square to the next, she considers out loud who needs a house of which size.

"Too *big*," she says with clear irritation, as I offer up the closest doll as the tile house's next resident. We search and search again, like Goldilocks with her three beds, for the stuffed elephant whose trunk would suit the walls of the house just right.

It's the precision of her search that surprises me, the fact that she seems so concerned over these animals that she can't bear to squash a foot or crimp an ear. It is a sort of love she shows for them, albeit basic—a care for others, concern for their comfort and safety, in which she can practically forget herself.

At dinnertime, I catch her sneaking glances back to the couch, where she's laid the animals out in clumped-up order—soft dinosaurs with hard plastic lions, and plastic people with their zoological counterparts—waiting to get back and attend to them. If she finishes early—or convinces us she's done with dinner, bending down, turning her head—she rushes back to the couch to feed them leftovers, to ensure they won't go hungry, no matter what happens, that there will be some peas and pureed sweet potatoes left.

Her stroller is packed with creatures of all shapes and sizes—a plastic Sophie giraffe someone bought her from France, a few soft "monster bowling balls," with googly eyes and heads meant to be tapped. She wants to make sure that they'll all be fine, that none of them will feel left out or friendless or sad. When we're out, she inspects every dog we pass to see if they have any injury, whether they're happy or angry or want to go home.

The trips take twice as long as they should. At first, in a rush to get somewhere or other, I hurried her home, but now I try to allow us the time, try to allow myself to be surprised by what we might find. Never before have I been so attentive to dogs' paws and muzzles, to the way their owners bring them forward with a light step or tug on their leashes. It is love that makes exotic what we encounter, that lends a mysterious air to the four-legged creatures we've passed on the cobblestone streets, in various guises—wearing tiny sweaters, as is the trend in our South End neighborhood, or with expressions of desperation for springtime, as they raise one leg to relieve themselves on the mounds of mixed ice and snow, then trot along to the dog park, where they mingle with their doggy friends and chase balls and fight the poodles on a typical day.

Henry, the nineteen-year-old mutt in the neighbor's first-floor apartment, has just had to have surgery on his ear. "He's fragile," his owner tells her, as Sophie bends in for a pat. "Be careful with him." But she doesn't even have to say it—Sophie's already leaning over with an intense, fixed expression, a crinkle caught between her eyes, and giving him a full-on hug against his belly, careful to avoid his ear.

"He's sick," she proclaims. "To the doctor?" He did see the doctor, my neighbor says—and immediately, Sophie's looking into his eyes, the way she's seen the doctor do for her, putting her face right next to his big twitchy nose. In the end, it's she who needs to be consoled that he's doing all right, that he needs rest but doesn't need an extra dose of medicine.

One day it's dogs; the next day it's dinosaurs. In the Museum of Science, the enormous central dinosaur wears a red-and-white striped scarf that has her obsessed. "Is he *cold*?" she asks me, shivering herself, as if in unanticipated empathy. It is this empathy, directed outward and seemingly globally, for both human and nonhuman creatures, which fascinates me. It's an empathy that arises in the midst of all the typical preschooler behavior, and seemingly in spite of it—not listening when I ask her to pick up her toys, fighting her showers with an all-out squeal, even lunging out occasionally at her playmates when she's hungry, irritated, or tired.

Certainly she's not always on her best behavior, nor would I expect her to be—and it is that contradiction that most puzzles me. On the one hand, immersed in her two-year-old world of taking turns on the playground swings and learning (often with drawn-out tears) to share, she's very much what I would have expected. And yet, there is something deep and wise about her care for living things, those fish who stare back at her wordlessly from the aquarium's glass, the bugs that creep across the sidewalk that she warns me about ("Don't step, mama").

This empathy is mysterious in its origins—I wonder if it's learned from Philippe's and my small kindnesses in daily life. As we change her diapers and clean her cereal when it falls, perhaps we are teaching her about the way the world can be put back together, how care can, in big and small ways, help the lives of others improve. Or perhaps it's innate, at least partially, a drive toward caretaking that, when not stymied by experiences of violence or trauma, can be allowed to flourish and thrive. I wish I could discover where her empathy comes from—if I could, perhaps I could find a way to encourage it in others, to prevent the loss of empathy and compassion that's obvious across the world, and in my own neighborhood, in the daily news.

The specific target of her attention isn't as critical—it's the care for other creatures that draws her in, the impulse of care for the other that draws her out into the world, and by extension, draws me out as well. Her empathy ignites a global empathy in me—through watching her care for others, I find myself more attentive to strangers I see on the subway, for the expressions of suffering or anger I catch, in the early morning, in their eyes.

It could be easy to go overboard with this concern, running from one cause to another, trying to fix whatever problems arise—or, alternately, to stay at the level of "wondering" rather than action, to see the suffering in the world, feel a moment of worry or sadness, and then pass by. Either extreme would be a kind of cruelty, though certainly an unintended one.

And yet I'm hopeful that, in all of this talk of empathy, there's a middle ground, a space where we can care enough to act, but not so much as to become overly anxious or paralyzed. I'm hopeful that, through raising my own level of concern, of feeling for others, I can move beyond "weeping while reading the paper," as a blogger once put it, and find a way to do what I can, in large and small ways, in the world.

I didn't think the impulse to love, to be empathic, would come so early in Sophie's life. I wasn't sure how I thought it would come—there are as many theories of love as there are philosophers, ranging from Plato to modern times. The Ancient Greeks distinguished between six different types of love, including *eros* or erotic love; *agape*, or selfless love, which C. S. Lewis referred to as "gift love" and others have linked with the Buddhist idea of universal loving kindness; and finally, *storge*, or "natural affection." That last form of love is the love I would have assumed she and I would feel—but in the end, her love doesn't seem at all that simple. She seems to cross boundaries with it, using it as a tool of transformation to re-envision others and herself. Polar bears can have emotional lives like us, she seems to be saying—they too can freeze in the depths of a Boston winter, can be shocked out of their typical routines with the onrush of cold. Indeed they do, I'd later learn—while mostly solitary, they can have "well-developed friendships," according to zoologist Nikita Ovsianikov. In a world where we typically close in on ourselves, especially in winter—as one friend recently wrote, at this time of year, he hardly makes time to write e-mails—this outward affection and care seems critical. It's a reminder, to me, to find a way out of my own skin, to forget myself.

Perhaps it is *agape* that I see developing in Sophie, a love that cares for the human and nonhuman forms of life, a love that does not question whether one is "supposed" to love a stuffed monster or a fluorescent pink bear, affectionately named Mr. Bear and carted around from one city to the next. Or perhaps it is *ludus,* or playful love, often referred to as the love between young children—laced with affection and silliness, marked by an interest in imagining alternate roles. The rules of love are as fluid as the rules of play—a bear might as easily heal a wound as scale a mountain, and she herself becomes a pilot, a train conductor, or a mother bear.

This love may be connected to children's associative and cooperative play, as in Mildred Parten's stages of play development—as early as 1932, she distinguished between associative play, in which children are interested in engaging with others but not in an organized way, and cooperative play, a type of play that has rules and roles, such as children playing house.

As Sophie develops, she is beginning to travel through these stages just as I traveled across continents in the years prior to having her. As I watch her and carefully observe, I too am traveling through these stages, finding each one anew like a ripple in a river, like the next city on an impossibly long list. I come to realize how interconnected love is with play—how, in loving someone without any thought for one's own self-interest, we can allow them to transform into someone or something else. This is perhaps the ultimate gift to someone—the gift of allowing a person to reach outside of him or herself, to become transformed.

Sophie's love seems particularly characterized by empathy, the ability to "suffer in" and experience how another might be hurting. This empathy, arising from the small gestures of a child, can be connected to the religious traditions: Buddhism, with its emphasis on deep compassion, and Christianity, with its focus on feeling into the suffering of Christ. It has been the subject of much recent neuroscience research, with a focus on "mirror neurons" in understanding the brain's role in empathy. These neurons, which serve as a neural basis for sharing emotions (they fire both when a person acts and when he sees the same action performed by another), have been found to be especially busy in people who score high on tests of empathy. Perhaps empathy is only one element of the brain's furious making of connections, one that can be helped along or stymied through the

environment. But what about love? Recently, biologists have suggested that it has a genetic basis, along with an element of nurturing programmed from the womb. Even from birth, children can distinguish their mother's voice from a stranger's based on nine months of training from inside.

And yet the reason for love's development seems hard to determine. It isn't, strictly speaking, necessary, except (as evolutionary psychologists theorize) as a mode of attachment helping to ensure the togetherness of mother and child. It's a strange contradiction—at some level, love seems fluffy or superfluous, the subject of nursery rhymes and romantic songs, while at another level, it responds to our most cherished inner longing, our deepest biological need.

Before having a child, I had taken its existence for granted, but clearly, it's not as simple as that. What most modern theories have in common is that *love requires love*—that is, for a child to develop feelings of care and concern for others, she must first be the recipient of care herself. The impulse to nurture others thus arises from a prior experience of having been nurtured. Thus, in a way, I can see her deep impulse to care for others as evidence that she's felt cared for and loved herself. Cruelty, in contrast, can be understood as often arising from a lack of love or care early in life—for example, Alberich in Wagner's Ring Cycle, who is denied love and ends up stealing the Rhinegold, or Silas Marner, who is framed for a crime and cast off in marriage, and ends up hoarding his gold.

As for myself, I've grown into my own empathy in a way that continues to surprise me. Prior to having Sophie, I had dreams about what she would look like—enhanced by the ultrasound's blurry images of a curled-up nose—but could hardly envision any specifics. My love for her felt floating, unable to settle, no matter how many times I walked into the nursery or stared at the piles of baby clothes. My identity too felt wavering, uncertain, driven equally by an anticipation of love as by fear. In a world that I navigated too often through the use of rationality, the newness of a child could feel overwhelming, like the answer to a question I had yet to pose. I had fears about not knowing what she would look like, dreams of realizing she was a monster and I was too, and no matter what we did, we could never be transformed back into ourselves.

Luckily, my fears of monstrous births went unrealized. I think back to the moment she Sophie was first born—"she's adorable," I said, seeing her face, exhausted as mine, popped with the hint of a smile. Her eyes were shut as tight as a newborn lamb's.

I didn't think about the unrelenting nights of waking every two and a half hours that would soon follow. I didn't think about the worries we'd face even in her early years, the sudden spike of a fever that made my already high-alert anxiety heighten as we rushed to the hospital at midnight. Nothing, we later found out, was the matter, other than a virus that would abate on its own. I didn't think about the sicknesses she'd pile on before even starting preschool.

In those moments, I felt the archetypal fear of every mother—the fear that we'd missed the window to help her, that my love for her wasn't backed by action quickly enough. Looking back, I see it was ridiculous, a first-time mother's panic over a minor discomfort. It's the same panic that had me bringing her in to the doctor after six week's time, when I found that nothing I could do, other than carry her in her purple sling, would calm her down. The doctor's office, of course, was the first time in three days she lay quiet, at peace.

The doctor, an older woman with coiled brown hair, listened to my description of the "problem," nodding her head occasionally when I described my long walks down the frozen sidewalks to soothe her, my attempts to use the bathroom with one hand, bouncing her with the other, my exhaustion when the two of us finally slept. *I must have really carried on*, I can think now. The doctor must have seen hundreds of babies, many more premature than mine.

"I think I know what it is," she said with a half-smile, turning to face me. Sophie, for the first time in three weeks, cooed.

"Yes?" I smiled, happy to see it, but embarrassed to have so little evidence for my *she cries all the time* claim.

"I diagnose her with . . . being a baby," she said, patting my shoulder.

"Not even colic?"

"No—she's done a pretty good job of soothing herself here. Many babies at her age can't do that. You're one of the lucky ones, if you can believe it."

"Yes?" I said.

"Yes," she repeated.

"Sure." I did my best to try to convince myself.

After that, I retell that story to myself and to Philippe whenever I start to feel worried about what Sophie has, about what's wrong with her. I tell the story to remind myself that love doesn't have to involve worry, that I can let go of my impulse to fix her problems and, in most cases, let us learn together, and understand and love one another through play. Love for a child, in many ways, feels opposite of a grasping, needy love, and much more like the need to let go.

This letting go, for me, has been a lesson when I start to feel panicked about how well she's doing, when I start to feel the need to control. I'm reminded of my time at the speech clinic, where I had to listen closely and learn not to speak over what someone was trying to say. "You ask too many questions," I remember my supervisor saying, after observing me stumbling to find out about a patient's background. "Remember, these patients have trouble getting words out. That's why they're here. You need to ask them one question, then wait. Give them time."

She was teaching me, even back then, I realize, about how to manage a selfless form of love, how to reach beyond one's own fear and nervousness to offer the other what he or she needs. It is that form of love that is careful about projecting one's own emotions and needs onto someone else, that allows time and space and opportunities for the other to speak. Love, in this way, becomes a form of making room for the other, encouraging another's growth and expansiveness. This care may be for a patient or for a child—in either case, it is a form of love that allows for both internal and external journeys, that manages to coexist with danger, with careful but intentional daring, with the chance for failure. She was teaching me to risk it—since without risk, there is nothing to be learned. It is through this risk—and the chance for failure—that we learn to love. It is this risk that makes our love more meaningful.

❖ ❖ ❖

Peace Park

You notice the silence,
the absence of city sounds in this city center.
You notice the vast stretches of grass
and openness to the sky, the few trees
in full fall color. You notice the beauty
of the river as it meanders under the bridge.
You learn the bridge was the target.
You see the single, hollowed-out
shell of a building, the epicenter,
and memorials in the distance.
People around you speak in hushed tones
as if in a church. You see groups
of uniformed schoolchildren
learning what you are learning:
the randomness of destruction,
how this city was chosen
because it was sunny that day,
like New York on 9/11,
because Kyoto was cloudy.
You find the phrase *Never Again*
etched in stone, repeat it to yourself
over and over.
                    And then
you go with your son,
whose grandfather that day
was on a warship
steaming toward this coast,
and your daughter-in-law,
whose grandfather
defended this same coast,
and together you share
okonamiyaki, the special pancakes
Hiroshima was famous for
before it was famous for this.

Carol V. Davis

White Nights

Midnight could be noon, people strolling
on the Embankment unable or unwilling
to tell the difference. Drunken song and linked arms.
But it is January I love, when night tucks in the corners
of the city with piles of snow pushed against the curb.
The blinking lights of the blini café, the samovar's
breath puffing against the front window.
Walking back from the metro, blackness presses against
the Soviet block apartments until they are indistinguishable.
Darkness untamed even in this major metropolis.
The day I took the wrong minibus, ended far from the city,
the fear of never getting back, picturing my wool coat
curled beneath the birches, a small animal.
Not that the bus left me so far out, but alone
on a road, past a half-frozen lake, a shabby church
with a midnight cupola, no English in sight.
I crossed the road, stamped my feet to keep from numbing,
a prayer to keep my tongue from losing its agility.
A man pulled a sled piled with firewood on a path
that was no path.
And I waited.

Kelly Fordon

How Slowly the Brain Registers

Snow-coated trampoline, how
frosted the steely chair of you, slowly
slippery sidewalk, the breath clouds, the
fringe of white in your beard at the root, brain
shifting, sodden, lodged between ice floes, registers
the shy steps you take so as not to fall, the words, the
stick in your throat, (the ones you can't find—*end
freeze*) everyone will try to make you feel better, this is
how you'll know, this is the catch, they'll say, winter is near,
they'll say one more freeze, thirty more days, if only, how
is your tomorrow? you believed them once, twice, more slowly
now, maybe it was many winters ago, you dragged your sled up the
biggest hill, you flew down that hill, disregarding the probability of brain
damage, you didn't need mittens, or a hat, you never said, *How registers
it outside? or* . . . Sometimes when the sidewalks were slick, you stayed in the
the middle of the road, hot cocoa was reason enough to venture out, but no end
to inside now, heat turned up to manipulate molten glass, fingers blue with cold, is
this even the indoors? Is this the great blizzard of *you only live once*, or not so near?

The Hole

The winter his wife died he said there's a hole in the world.
Yet a hole does not scare.
Let hole stay as it is. And where.
Not repair.
Does a hole grow hair? Smudge at the margins
like a charcoal drawing?
Does hole have walls? Echo like a cave?
Is hole heated?
Can he live there in some comfort?
How does one tend a hole?
Flush it out with a garden hose?
Cold water? Or warm?
What if all its densities thinned
and hole were to become elegant as a pencil.
A hole to be wished for. Courted even.
Can hole widen or narrow?
Make funny faces. Sing like a canary.
Can hole count?
Reckon the sum of its own absence?
Does hole have a belly.
Can hole eat around its own edges.
Take a stance on religious questions.
Is hole a hole forever.
Or does it change with chance? With the weather?
Whenever it damn well feels like it.
Can hole dance? Can it reason?
Is hole risqué? Or decent?
Does hole believe in God. Is hole God.
Does it scream. Dream.
Think holy or unholy thoughts.
Is hole honest?
Wholly authentic?
Sometimes he speaks to it. Sometimes hole listens.
Sometimes hole talks back.

A Daughter's Villanelle

For poetry makes nothing happen. . . .
                    –W. H. Auden

This trifling scheme, these little skips of rhyme
are all you know to do. Ream out your brain
while what she's going through should strike you dumb.

Yet on you patter in this foolish form
French peasants danced to. Each breath's a refrain
of its own, needs no trifling scheme or rhyme.

Nor does she sing, but that she sings to him—
he then takes up the burden of her strain.
What they are singing through would strike you dumb

if you could hear it. In this sunny room
you'd think them young, with nothing to complain
of, nothing to be turned to scheme or rhyme.

Tune your own lyre. Your song is not for them
nor should it be. The theme they strum again
with expert fingers only makes you dumb.

She is your mother, hers the mother-womb
all your words come from, yet no words explain
what she is going through. It'd strike you dumb.
What's left you now to do but scheme and rhyme?

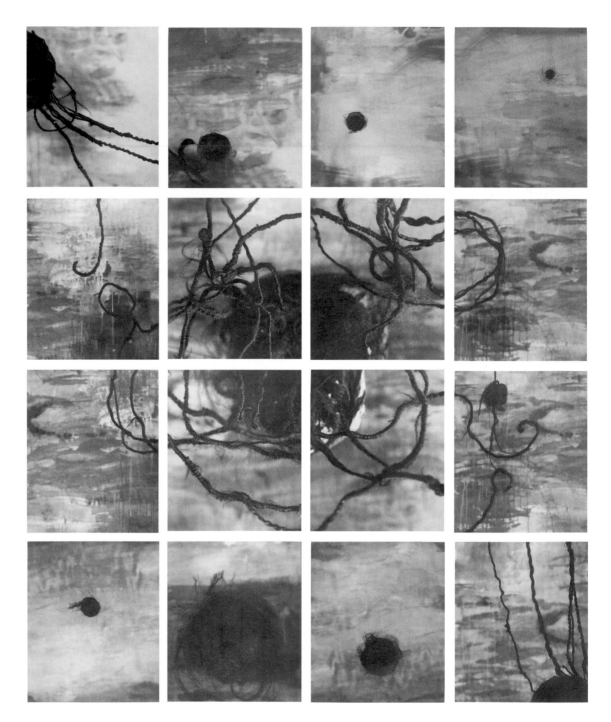

María Magdalena Campos-Pons, *Constellation*, 2004, instant color prints, Smithsonian American Art Museum, Museum purchase through the Luisita L. and Franz H. Denghausen Endowment. © 2004, María Magdalena Campos-Pons. Reproduced courtesy of Museum of Fine Arts, St. Petersburg, from "Our America: The Latino Presence in American Art."

Jack Bushnell

Writing on Water

In mid-February, I come upon two sets of fox prints, trotting in parallel across a wide creek near my home. Though both are small, one measures slightly larger, probably the male. It's likely at this time of year that the female is already pregnant and that they've established a den somewhere nearby. Within a couple of months they'll have kits, and by the end of summer they'll all have scattered to live solitary lives until next January or so. But for now these two move together, unhurriedly, on the lookout for mice or rabbits or a careless bird. The story of their year has only begun, and as I stand over it, on the ice and snow in the middle of the frozen creek, I am struck most by its simplicity. Hunting for food, heading toward shelter, patrolling territory, the endlessly repetitive, largely uneventful rounds of a life. Animals in the wild are either profoundly interesting or profoundly dull, depending on your perspective. I happen to hold both views, which is perhaps why I so much enjoy reading tracks. They are spots of time, fragments of lives, ephemeral but resonant in the delightful manner of a short story or poem, available only until the next snowfall, or until the spring melt turns them to water and rushes them away downstream.

So I pay attention and stay put for a while, trying to notice everything I can. Just around the next bend I find the characteristic bounding pattern of a river otter, two footprints side by side, then a lengthy space, then two footprints side by side, and so on, along one stretch of the creek ice. All of the weasel family move like this, and there has been some decaying of the tracks since the animal passed this way, but the size of the stride and of the feet makes me reasonably certain it's an otter. A heron was here too, perhaps looking for a fishing hole. And I see a loping, dog-like set of prints, too large for a fox, too small for a wolf. Maybe it really was just a dog, from one of the houses at the edge of this county forest. Maybe a

coyote. The prints are old and indistinct, so I can't guess with any confidence. But I like the process. Walking out here in the middle of the creek, my tracks mingling with the others, I try to fill in the gaps of the stories before me. Where were they going? Where had they come from? What were they doing?

If you gaze about you in a snow-muffled forest, your strongest impression is of peace, calm, stasis. Except for the occasional chuckle of a woodpecker or the monotonous call of a chickadee, nothing much seems to be happening. And this is largely true; nothing much *is* happening. But it *was*. For if you look to the ground when you're in the woods, at all those intersecting, wayward tracks, the impression is of almost *antic* activity. Rabbits, squirrels, mice, deer, weasels, foxes, birds. Well-trodden trails or fresh single tracks. It's as if I'm seeing all of these animals at the same time, in the present, like travelers in a giant train station, all crossing each others' paths, heading off in various directions, living their separate lives, foraging for food and water, killing, dying, eating, defecating, together, alone. These stories in a quiet wood can be a little overwhelming. They are loud and bustling and often hard to read. At the same time, however, they are wispy and unreal, for the animals I "see" exist only as traces of the past, of the already gone, unsubstantial as ghosts.

❖ ❖ ❖

Unlike the other animals in my life, all the household dogs, cats, and hamsters, the chickens we raised when I was a child, the rabbits in their hutches, the snakes in their terrariums, even the injured field mice we nursed back to health before letting them go again—unlike these animals that I fed and cared for and loved, the animals of the wild haunt me. Those I don't see, have never seen, and quite likely will never see hold an allure that all my gentle, good pets cannot hope to match.

Is it because we humans tend to desire what we don't and can't have? Is it because we generally consider wild animals worthier than those we domesticate? Pets are always there, always around, steady, dependable. Wild creatures by definition are not. They are animals of the imagination. Their very evasiveness, their foreignness, makes them hard to resist. But it's more than that. For me, it's the feeling that they've left me a message, that they've written me an invitation . . . to join them. And they've added a nearly invisible P.S.: they do not promise to be there when I arrive.

❖ ❖ ❖

Spring is the best time to explore the banks of rivers and creeks, for most animals in a forest make their way to water sometime during the day, and they leave the evidence of their visits in the wet sand or mud. A few weeks ago, before the trees and scrub had begun to leaf out here in Wisconsin, and while it was still relatively easy to hike upstream through the woods, I walked a stretch of the south fork of one of the large rivers in the western part of the state. I was in the neighborhood of a small wolf pack, one I'd trailed previously only in winter snow, mostly along logging roads two or three miles west of here. I hoped now to spot some of their prints near the water. As it turned out, I saw no wolf sign, but I saw plenty of other activity, a seeming congress of geese, ruffed grouse, rabbit, mice, possible mink, raccoons, deer, stepping in each others' tracks, approaching the water, leaving the water, not at the same time but within minutes of each other. Of course, none of them were here now, but I could see them just the same.

What I noticed first as I came down from the trees onto a bar, were the shuffling marks of an opossum through loose, dry sand. It dragged its feet as it walked, creating two lines of busy whorled prints. Between them, its tail cut a clear, continuous furrow. I followed it to the water, then back up to the top of the sandbar, where it continued its perambulation upstream. I saw no indications of hunting or foraging; as far as I could tell, this was just a midnight stroll. Not so with the raccoon prints I encountered at the river's edge. They suggested a systematic search for food, a digging here and there, a detour into a partially submerged debris pile of branches and grass washed down from upriver, a foray into the water for a distance, then back onto the bank, the little hand-like prints of its forefeet inscribing a soundless patter in the sand. I followed this animal along at least a couple of wide sweeps of the stream before I saw its path veer toward the trees, head into a small pool on the beach, rake a deep trough in the gravelly bottom there, and continue on. Several feet further, the open shell of a large freshwater clam, the inside still wet with bloody residue. In that pool, the raccoon had finally found something to eat, had pried it apart and scooped it out. A lot of time and energy for one clam, but what I noted above all was the disparity in the dual stories I'd been tracking. The opossum with no clear intentions, just a meandering along the top of the bar. The raccoon working the river, working the sand, alert for signs of prey. Two omnivorous mammals heading upstream, more or less in the same place at the same time, but quite separate, probably unaware of each other or, if aware, keeping their distance.

Oddly, it's the distance I feel most strongly. Not just the space between animal and animal, but between the animals—all of them—and me. One of the pleasures I get from tracking derives from deciphering the "mysteries of nature," that is, quite simply finding out what's going on when I'm not there. A wood turtle carapace, for example, near the water, its yellow plastron largely intact, the shell hollowed out long ago, likely the victim of a skunk, raccoon, or opportunistic coyote. Had it hunkered down in the sand to protect itself? How long had the predator circled it, looking for an opening? Or, on a different day, under big, overhanging cottonwood trees, I see deep, narrow holes dug along a creek in a wildlife preserve east of where I live. Crayfish are an important part of a raccoon's diet, and the prints around the holes tell me a 'coon was busy that night, snatching at the buried crustaceans while trying to avoid getting its fingers pinched. Or another day, another creek, the larger tracks of a fisher walking to the water's edge, sporadic marks of a tail drag as it crouched to drink. Or on the river again, I find scat up in the grass of the overhanging bank, full of fish scales and crayfish shell. An otter's sign. These encounters make me feel as if I've been let in on something very personal, a story for which I may be the sole reader. They give me the illusion of having occupied the space of the animal, even briefly, of having shared its experience, seen the world through its eyes, for a moment.

But this is only an illusion. For though reading signs may seem to be about connection, what tracker and author Tom Brown calls a "communion" with the "being" whose prints you follow, more often it is about *dis*connection, about arriving too late to witness the very thing you now work so hard to re-create in your mind. It's about shadows and scuff marks, symbols in the sand, fresh and clear and beautifully formed. And empty. Though we may generally share the same three dimensions of space, this animal and I, we do not share the fourth dimension, time. Thus, five minutes may as well be five hundred miles, for all the closeness they bring us. It's like trying to catch the current that, even as you think you're watching it, has already slipped away.

Whenever I track along a stream, I can't help wondering what I'm missing on the other side. Which prints that I've never before seen are just over there, out of reach? Maybe a wolverine (very unlikely). Or a cougar (ditto). Which exotic animal will have come that close to me without my ever knowing it? Rivers, because of their width, offer only the rarest opportunities to cross, but creeks often provide natural bridges, trees that have fallen when the banks eroded beneath them, some of those trees still alive, growing horizontally, their roots firmly embedded, their branches leafy and strong. I take advantage of these bridges, the thrill of balancing above the flow, the triumph of scrambling onto the opposite bank. And when I get there, I find more of the same. I walk crouched, examining this foot length, measuring that stride. I sketch in my notepad, jot a few observations, straighten up. There's the creek again, separating me from whatever is written across the way. I wonder what I'm missing, what I will have forever missed.

❖ ❖ ❖

Tracking is narrow work, like any kind of reading. Nose in book, eyes to ground, I neglect what's not on the page. Perhaps an owl lifting noiselessly from the branch, gliding into the forest. Or a mink bounding across the trail far ahead of me. Or the yellow eyes of a wolf deep among the trees. Those things *are* happening out there somewhere, probably close by. Shouldn't I be watching for them? Yet if I keep my gaze up, binoculars at the ready, I may overlook the only evidence of what went on in this section of the woods last night or early this morning. I might walk past those prints I'd most hoped to find and forfeit my chance to witness, in my mind's eye, the rich variety of activity here. So, on one level or another, I miss all of it. Which puts me back where I started. If tracking is about ghosts, the "seen" and the "unseen," about populating nature with creatures already in the past, then where is its substance? Where is its meaning? If it can offer me only hints of life, but rarely the flesh and bone of the living animal, then it is like the water of the river, gone the instant I dip my hand into it. At the end of the day, I leave with nothing physical, no graspable connection to the natural world whatsoever.

Yet—and here's the paradox—I don't leave empty-handed. When I follow an animal's tracks, I am reminded over and over that these are not empty woods, that when I'm not here countless creatures go about their daily routines, the sometimes dangerous, often tedious business of survival. More important, I realize they do so with absolutely no concern for me. They do not leave their nests, burrows, holes, or dens in order to perform for my benefit. They care nothing for my desire to sight something interesting, something unusual.

Though I have come upon dramatic scenes—an owl's wings etched in the snow where it had swooped down upon a small mammal; the remains of a fox, its backbone pulled out, its body cavity eaten clean—the fact is that these animals' lives (like our own) are mostly not all that interesting, not all that dramatic. Tracking teaches me to read and value the stories of life as it is lived day to day, as it *was* lived shortly before I came along to attend to it. It teaches me that what I see is not necessarily significant in the way I might originally have imagined, not necessarily "meaningful." There are no metaphors in those prints in the snow or mud, unless you consider their kinship with infinite numbers of other prints along the edges of infinite numbers of other rivers and creeks. In that context, from that perspective, they transcend us, as they should. Their narratives are intriguing precisely because they refuse to become ours. In the end (truth be known) what I often desire most is to be one of them, to get so close, to mingle so completely, that we are indistinguishable. I want to be wild. But these animals I follow will have none of it. They declare themselves separate from me at every step, absent in my presence. They leave me only the most transitory clues to what their lives are like. Yet I continue to reach for them across the divide between us, even as I know at best I'll end up only with shadows and ripples on a stream.

If tracking holds any meaning for me, that's it.

❖　❖　❖

Late April and early May: two days, two different creek bottoms, one with stretches of high banks full of swallows, the other low and muddy. Giant silver maples loom over one of the creeks, some with several main trunks rising from a single base, and I hear the staccato laugh all around me of pileated woodpeckers, calling, responding, occasionally flying free of the canopy, their white under-feathers and red topknots bright in the sun. Chorus frogs sound their raspy, continuous trill. Periwinkles scatter the forest edge. White-throated sparrows, juncos, finches, mallards, a winter wren, birds everywhere. The bank swallows swoop, hover, and scold me before fluttering back to their holes. All is lush and green and becoming impassable. But the other creek is worse, a tangle of scrub alder that hems me in, deer trails so low and narrow they drive me to my knees. I forget how different we are, how small and nimble the deer compared to me. I can't walk their path as they walk it. Close to the ground, I note the clumps of new fern shoots, their tops curled like the scrolls of fiddles. I watch the wolf spiders hurry through the leaf litter. I hear but cannot see a flock of angry jays; they've spotted me no doubt and clearly wish me to leave.

But what of the mammals I came looking for? I find their writing of course. Raccoons, mice, deer, rabbits, one coyote, all evidenced in the mud and wet sand, all caught briefly in the act of their passing. Yet the animals themselves are nowhere to be seen. And it is this very lack that spurs me on. Surrounded by a cacophony of life and song and movement, by the bursting of spring deep in a county forest, I turn my attention instead to the traces of creatures no longer present, to silent tales of nature at its simplest, at its most mundane and most compelling. I don't have much time; I'm chasing the past after all. But if I follow them for a while, perhaps I'll learn something. Or I'll remember something I already knew. These are the stories that lure me on, like shades of memory, like the water of the stream, curling around the far bend and out of sight.

❖　❖　❖

Elisabeth Murawski

Things to Tell the Grief Counselor

There's a hole in the window, jagged
and fresh. It lets in the light,
a draft of cold air. What broke
the glass? I see no stone

or child's ball. I do see a hand
not mine poking through. Caution:
it's a young hand. Any hand
can bleed. Beyond the glass the sky's

the pale gray silk of a Whistler
nocturne. Waking, I'm like a miner
working a difficult seam of ore.
Because I've had this dream before.

I remember it when I read Cavafy's poem
about windows that aren't there,
and why that could be a good thing—
to be spared the light.

Frank Romero, *Death of Rubén Salazar*, 1986, oil, Smithsonian American Art Museum, Museum purchase made possible in part by the Luisita L. and Franz H. Denghausen Endowment. © 1986, Frank Romero. Reproduced courtesy of Museum of Fine Arts, St. Petersburg, from "Our America: The Latino Presence in American Art."

Jericho

IT was the Saturday morning of another demolition ceremony. Daddy set his toolbox on the kitchen table. "Where are you going so early?" I asked.

He muttered something about fixing Juana Carson's set of closet doors.

If Daddy had it his way, he'd fix everyone's closet doors, and live his life out in this wreckage they call, *Cabrini Green*.

Jericho, he'd once preached it.

—And to hear him now, if you weren't paying attention you'd barely hear him. The voice going was the reason he'd given for leaving the pulpit. A man with once thunderous intonations, and to hear him his speak as worn and gravely as sandpaper, or to see him in his unkempt appearance, bib overalls and broken straps, no one would never think he was a man on the good side of the Lord. Once a vibrant young boy, coming all the way from Mississippi to Chicago at the time the history books called the *Great Migration of Southern Blacks*, they came to get away from Jim Crow, where up North, a Southern black man could surely take it up a peg or two, and my daddy, just itching to be a pastor, was no exception.

So tucked into the land of public housing, in a little Baptist church, he'd found his Glory.

However, my older brother and Daddy's only son, Roy, was killed. Nicknamed by the Larrabee gang "Trailer," because when he was little, he'd trail behind the older boys, stomping on the heads of their shadows, he himself had made it to the ripe old age of twenty-five, and when my daddy left the pulpit, he'd literally said, "The hell with you." Not to me, of course. God, he meant it, too.

It'd been close to two years now, and it still saddened me that my daddy, the Pastor Edwin Ford, hadn't returned to the pulpit, riding back on his heels ready to preach the day.

❖ ❖ ❖

That morning I'd made him coffee and told him that he ought to sit down and have something to eat. He rattled through his toolbox not paying any attention. After he'd stopped his preaching, he started collecting small, indiscriminate hand tools, spending all his days fussing about the buildings, fixing things, some things not even broken.

Seeing his left eye with weeping, I got up, grabbed a towel off the oven handle, wrapped an end around my finger, and dabbed gently the corner of his eye.

"Daddy? You know that they're knocking down another building today?"

"Where'd you put my long screwdriver?" he asked, pushing the towel away.

I threw the hand towel into the kitchen sink. Scared a small black spider up the kitchen wall.

"Daddy," I said, "it's not always about your tools."

"It's about you taking my long screwdriver."

He just sat there fondling his instruments of healing, and I wasn't quite sure what mood he was in.

I pulled opened the narrow drawer and rummaged through slender odds-and-ends, then felt the long metal shank. "Look, Daddy," I said, slamming it on the kitchen table. "I found your screwdriver."

He groaned. "There's my long screwdriver. I knew you kept it from me." He wiped his hands on the sides of his overalls. "What other of my goddam tools have you been hiding?"

"Daddy, don't curse," I said, elevating my eyebrows to show him that he'd taught me right. "I wonder if Mama hears you curse like that."

He pulled a red handkerchief out from the back pocket of his overalls, and wiping the tool clean, he muttered, "Don't you mind any, she hears."

I had to ask. "Daddy, are you going to the demolition ceremony?"

Nose down, he thought for a moment, and muttered, "Ceremony?"

"I told you that they're tearing down a building today. Everybody's gonna watch."

He tossed the screwdriver into his toolbox. "Well, I aint."

We'd always enjoyed a pretty good relationship. So that said, at sixty-four, he was already a tired old man—wooly hair, balding with patches of gray like briar; blotchy russet skin; big brown eyes, but glazed and pink-rimmed, constantly teary from his persistent melancholy and allergic sensitivity to mold and pollen—and I hadn't expected him to become so bullheaded.

"Daddy," I said. "You know it's time we start looking. Got the paper right here."

"It's time you bring me some coffee," he replied. I poured him a mug. He took it. Puckered his lips, blew across the top, sipped once. "This here coffee is weak."

I went over to the coffeepot, pulled it off its warming plate, and emptied it into the sink. I held my breath just as I did when I wore pigtails in my hair and my mamma was alive giving me what for. Counting off, I released my breath, and with a heavy sigh said, "You know they's eventually gonna tear the whole place down."

I knew he'd loved me, but he sat there, silent, not realizing that the world around him was changing, and he looked around the apartment, into the corners, under tables, behind chairs, one eye weepy shut—and he asked, "Where else you've been hiding my tools?"

I gave up. "I'll fix you some toast," I said, feeling him slip away.

He rubbed his hand over his face.

"I gots to tend to some broken closets."

We don't talk much about Roy, not since him stealing from the cash register on a night too dark and too cold to even think about moving, let alone rob a nearby convenience store. I remember to this day, hearing the alarm bell ringing out followed by the shot that took him from us. A CHA officer had chased him through Cabrini. Roy might have been running home or away. We'd never know because he was shot in the back. Gunned down. Fell right outside of our building on Larrabee Street. All the excuses Daddy had given. But the real reason he'd stopped his

preaching was because that shot had also gone through him. It'd torn him apart. Saw it first in his eyes, and then in his soul, and slowly he'd detached. The way paint, weathered against the light, cracks and peels away.

My father, my mama, my brother, and many of my relatives before had lived here, and don't get me wrong, I'm grateful for the buildings coming down. In fact, the dust and rubble supported my cause to leave it all behind. Some memories included.

Downing his cup of coffee, he grabbed his toolbox.

"What about your toast?"

It was going to be a nice day, skies clear, and as he got up to leave, I reminded him that we were going to look at some of these places starting tomorrow. Then flashing the newspaper, I shouted, "And you're not getting out of it."

He looked scared, a gravedigger's look. Standing at the door, so much he says these days, comes without words. I was frightened for him, especially that day, and I told him that he didn't have to do everything everybody tells him. It was too much work for him to go around and pick up trash or fix people's broken faucets. They just take advantage of him, of his grief and sacrifice, of his pain and weakness, and if I don't watch him, he'd work himself to death. Those moments sicken me and I hate my brother for getting himself killed.

Daddy walked out not telling me how long he'd be gone, and I called out, "Will you be home for lunch?"

He poked his head back through the door. "I know you never think that I'll be back."

I ate the toast and continued looking through the listings.

❖ ❖ ❖

I'd been meaning to give my boyfriend, Theo, my answer to his question. To be honest, I hadn't expected to take this long. I've been all on the fence about it, and it wasn't like he asking came as a surprise. I'd known him most my life, and together we've been through the thick of things. But I guess it was just hard now, seeing it all crumble around us. Like sandcastles meeting their match in a big wave, and I'm not sure what to make of it. The damage, I mean.

In my mind I was prepared to marry him, but in my heart, I wanted to go it on my own. I'd recently finished Harold Washington City College with a degree in business administration and had just accepted a job, my first real job, and at twenty-five, the same age of my brother, I was on my way of putting the whole subsidized package behind me—the Title-8 housing, college aid, city clinics, food stamps, and where we lived, Cabrini Green—and though it was the only home I'd ever known, no matter how much love had spattered on the old red brick—there comes a time to move on.

And if Daddy weren't so dependent on me, this place, I would have moved out long ago. Maybe on my own. Maybe already married.

It was a dream. The Housing Authority said if you're married, have good jobs, and stay clean for over a year, then you have first dibs. Although the deal worked like a lottery and it wasn't considered a handout. The new townhouses were for those who lived in public housing wanting out, but each day, the longer we stay, the lower our chances of realizing the dream. All around us, rows and rows of vacant buildings, tall grass brush against twenty-storied concrete towers. We'd have to move quickly or be left out in the cold. Marriage was the answer. And if I don't make my decision, soon, not just the buildings will topple.

❖ ❖ ❖

Preparing Daddy's lunch, I pulled out some slices of baloney and grabbed the sack of bread.

I had nightmares. Some nights I'd wake in a sweat with my heart pounding. A dream I'm running around the neighborhood, winded and huffing, with my fingers stuffed in my ears, stopping the ringing.

The night sky was purple like a bruise. Streetlights, small buds of yellow light the size of Chiclets.

I'd cut across a grassy field. The wet smell of grass lights the night air. The pool at Stanton Park, emptied, a pit of darkness. The Rec Building with its large mural—Black faces, young happy faces peeled and pocked—edges my path. I leap across a stretch of chopped-up sidewalk, and find, not my brother, but my father against a chain-link fence that surrounds the boarded-up church. A leather shoe stuck in a link. My daddy, arms spread wide, wrists threaded through the chains, hangs like the crucified Lord on Calvary.

I lift him up onto his feet and hold him around his waist. Pulling away, he tries to struggle free, but I kiss him on his wet cheek. We stand there for a minute, feet slip-sliding on the crumpled ground.

Legs, too, buckling like strands of wet noodles.

❖ ❖ ❖

Looking out the window, I saw that people were already gathering across the street. Daddy was late. I went up two flights of stairs to Juana's apartment. Before I knocked, the door opened. "Oh," the woman said, startled.

"Is my daddy here?" I asked.

She clutched the door with long and curling fingernails painted a deep shade of raisin. In her other hand she held a platter of chocolate cake.

I suspected that it was Juana Carson. She was younger than I'd imagined. Her hair was cropped into a short Afro, more Lauryn Hill than Halle Berry. Big brown eyes like two cups of black coffee, and she was wearing a silky blue warm-up.

"Jamila, right?"

"Yes, mam."

"Why he was here, but he left, and I was just on my way to bring this cake down to the wrecking."

"Cake?"

She backed from the door. "Come on in," she said, balancing the double-layer, chocolate-frosted cake in one hand.

The unit was identical to ours and she had the same view of the tall buildings across. Hers, though, cluttered with toys, smelled good of baking. Her two children, lying on the couch in front of the television, jumped off when they'd noticed me, making a path to their mother, tugging on her pant leg, wanting to know who the lady was.

"C'mon babies," she said. "Go watch some more TV." She lifted the cake platter high overhead as the two sprinted back to the TV and the cartoon playing. Once they were settled, she sat the platter down on the kitchen counter.

"Your daddy has been so good to us," she said "Don't know what I'd do without him." Her heels clacked on the linoleum. "Lemme get something to cover this."

"Please, mam." I stopped her. "Daddy say where he was going?"

She looked at me puzzled. "I reckon the building celebration. He was a bit riled about it all coming down."

Suddenly, there was a loud crashing sound on the television and the two kids started belly laughing and rolling.

Juana grabbed her throat, startled. "Every time I hear a loud crash my heart jumps to my throat."

I wasn't sure what to say. Juana's attention quickly diverted to her kids and she yelled at them to turn down the TV. She then looked at me with those big eyes, feathered eyelashes, and decaying mascara. " . . . Shit, if my kids get hold of this cake, they'll be off the walls."

The second loud noise came from outside—an ear-rattling explosion causing Juana to scream and her kids to cry and also startling me. I raced over to the window to see what'd happened.

The sky turned a smoky haze. A gnarled and grey cloud rose from the tower directly across the street.

Already, the wrecking ball was mounting a sizable force, coming over me like distant thunder, closer, louder. I slid open the window to the cheers from spectators lining on the street. My fear turned quickly to elation, seeing the building split and tear at the seams.

Juana came to the window with me. "Oh dear, they already started," she said, rattled. "I don't like big noises, not one bit."

I had to go and thanked her.

Heading to the door, she called me back.

"Listen, if you're gonna go down, can you take them this cake? My nerves are shattered."

She then handed it to me, and it wasn't until I was halfway down the stairs that I noticed it was still uncovered.

❖ ❖ ❖

My longtime friend Jessica Watkins was just outside. Younger, she'd do splits on the street corner and ruin her britches, then hand them down to me. Didn't ever want them and threw them away.

I asked her if she'd seen my father. "Girl, what's with the cake?" she asked. "We supposed to bring food?"

Before I could say no, she began recalling some old times, like the lockout by the Housing Authority one summer and how we all slept outside, and with a short laugh, she said, "Remember, how Roy would always lock himself out at night?" She had a big crush on my brother. And she was the one that'd once told me, if I married, it would be more out of pity than love. It'd shaken my confidence a bit.

"That wrecking ball do its job," I said, rushing away. "Soon there won't be a Housing Authority."

I left her and heard her yell, "Hey, are you going to share any of that cake?"

The crowd that'd gathered across the street was deep and applauding the strikes against the building. Daddy wasn't with them, but Theo was there, watching the demolition through the fence. He didn't see me. His fingers like claw hooks in the chin link. He was engrossed, as were the others who cheered. They'd fist-pump each striking blow. For me, seeing the building crumble with little resistance, I could no longer imagine how it'd ever stood for so long. The air tasted like chalk. Windows out like missing teeth. White specks snowing on the brown frosting, and I noticed that the convenient store Roy had robbed was already gone—nothing but broken asphalt and dandelions crept in—and I was the first to come to my brother's side. They said he'd stopped running and turned towards the officer, aimed a gun. He was shot, unconscionable, unimaginable, in the chest. The whole ordeal seemed like a dream that'd reoccurred over and over again, like now, one more building, like a giant beanstalk, falling from out of the sky.

I came up to Theo not realizing I was still holding the cake. "Who's that for?" he asked.

"No one," I said. "Have you seen Daddy?"

A couple pushed a baby stroller behind two women sitting in lawn chairs with a cooler between them.

He was wearing a red bandana on his head, matching the bright color of his Air Jordans. Shirtless, a pair of new jeans sagging low, just the crenellated waistband of his white boxers hugged his narrow hips. He was not shy and liked to stand out. "You see them knocking that one down? How many blows you think it'd take? It's like what Foreman got from Ali."

"I asked you if you've seen Daddy?"

"How . . . 'cause you haven't given me your answer?"

"I'd told you I needed some time, and now isn't it."

"I'm just wondering," he said, turning on his soft, gentle features. "If you're gonna let the Pastor dictate the rest of your life?" He still called my father "Pastor," out of a habit, ever since we were children attending church.

"I aint wedded to my daddy."

"Baby, I'll stand till you come to your senses or the city dumps this damn building right down on me." He then pulled out a housing pamphlet from his pocket and waved it in the air. I tried maneuvering away, but the cake was slipping. "Picture it, babe . . . we get married, one of 'em new houses is rightly ours."

Best I ignored it. Seen everyone flashing the pamphlet around. "You know they make you take drug tests."

He laughed as if I was kidding. "Baby, you know I've been clean since—"

"You telling me you're gonna hold down your job?"

"You know I love you. Always have, since we were, what? This high."

I didn't have to look to see his hand float just a few feet from the cracked sidewalk.

"Put your pamphlet back. Daddy should be here."

He shoved it into his back pocket. "You know, it's been two years since Trailer died, and you still haven't gotten your own life."

Theo had also called my brother, Roy "Trailer." He was like a record of the past that'd play over and again. Yet there we were, and never before had I been this inconsiderate. Not giving him my decision, especially when we'd been together for as long as I could remember, was reprehensible to say the least.

We'd known each other since we were sixth-graders attending Schiller Public School, dated seriously since sophomores at Wells High. He had more than enough faults. There were times I'd have to pick him up from detox at McDermott, and together we'd ride the El back to Cabrini-Green, and he'd say it was last time, sounding so convincing that every time I'd be-

lieve him. Now, like Jessica had once warned, I'm afraid that I love him just out of pity. His problem was crack cocaine, something easily gotten in the projects. Like fleas or bad advice. And I still saw him as that skinny fourteen-year-old kid—the one time—soaked head to toe, T-shirt and shorts shrink-wrapped to his boney frame, smiling bigger than a slice of the moon after he'd figured out how to release the water from a fire hydrant on a stifling day in Chicago. Not the young man he'd claimed to be. Ready to settle down, take on a mortgage, kids. Dog, maybe. But I didn't think.

However, I was ready to give him my answer. "Look, Theo . . ."

Just then, another thunderous strike of the iron ball rocked us. But this time the crowd, not applauding, gasped and screamed. Looking around, I saw the two women in the lawn chairs were standing, pointing up towards the top story of the building.

"Hey, ain't that the pastor?" Theo shouted.

Dammit. It was my father.

Leaning out of a top window of the seven-story building, he started yelling and raising his hands. I couldn't hear him. Nobody could. A jumbo jet crossed overhead. People started calling for the crazy man to jump. The baby in the stroller started crying. The foreman yelled to stop the wrecking ball. I ran by the fence near him. "That's my father."

He turned. "What's with the cake?"

"That's my daddy up there. Let me in."

He opened the gate, and I ran in. "Hold on, miss."

"I have to get him." I was hysterical, I think, threatening him with the cake. As frantic as I was, I'd caught him off-guard.

"You got to have a hat." He grabbed one off another worker's head and slammed it onto mine.

We got inside the building and ran up the stairwell. He followed, huffing and puffing. Our steps echoed as if we were shattering the icy emptiness with a pickax. When we got to the seventh floor, I screamed, "Which one, which one," whirling in circles with the cake balanced in one hand.

"That one." Out of breath, pot-bellied, his hands on his knees, he let me go inside by myself.

Sirens whined in the distance. First like infants; then mad seagulls.

Daddy was sitting on the floor below the window. His shoulders were curled. His face was soiled, but it was beautiful to me. I'd seen it strong and full of life. There'd been a day when Daddy, behind the pulpit, stood clean-shaven and purposeful. A little girl seated in the front pew, I'd sit close enough to smell his lemony aftershave rising off his chin. Mama's to my left and she smells sweet and flowery. She's wearing her church dress, a green cotton dress with a big ostrich feather in her felt hat. It waves in the breeze from the ceiling fan whirling above us. Roy's to my right, in tie and jacket, and he's looking up at Daddy smiling big. They're all saying Roy will be following in his daddy's footsteps. His voice is as strong and thunderous as Daddy's, who starts his sermon, "We don't walk alone." The congregation then goes crazy. Like lunatics, and starts whooping and howling amens and halleluiahs, and Daddy, the arsonist, is setting them on fire.

He'd always been more than a preacher, a caretaker gardening what little there was, nurturing some sense of sanity and hope, and I realized more now than back then, people draw strength from him, depend on him, love him.

And now, sitting on the floor, he winced in terror just at the sight of a cake.

I took my hard hat off. "How'd you get yourself up here?"

He did not move. Just sat there. His eyes riveted on the chocolate cake. You no more reveal secrets the deeper you look than press them tightly between your lips. So we no longer had to hide from them.

"Daddy, we couldn't hear you. What did you yell out the window?"

He looked at me. His face was gray with stubble and his eyes: the flame that'd flittered weak had gone out.

"Why they do it?" he cried. "Why the Good Lord let them take my son."

He started me crying. "It's ok, Daddy." I tried holding back a rush of my tears. "Here," I nervously chuckled. "I brought you some cake. Chocolate, your favorite."

He buckled flimsily at the waist, then moaned. "It hurts, baby girl. It hurts real bad."

Look at me, Daddy. My entire life I heard you like a trumpet's call, hung on your every word. So, Daddy Preacher, help me out now, restore the truth and rebuild my faith. Please say it so, Daddy. Please.

I heard footsteps coming and took his hand, squeezing until the bones gathered in mine. Then suddenly they came bursting through the door, leading with the nozzles of guns and ends of sticks, scaring the daylights out of us. And before they could say it. I'd thrown the cake. And, like the walls of Jericho, I swear, it caused the whole fucking thing to come a-tumbling down.

❖ ❖ ❖

Since all your friends

decided to sleep inside your body, you've had the plumbing to consider.
The picky ones expect their own rooms to engage in odd private acts.
These demands perplex the surgeon as she folds your dermis
and moves around your fat layers, forming a judgment about their abundance.
What scares you is not sharing yourself—you are used to it—
it's all the air your friends will exhale. It's how much air
you've shared, already. You might let them down by not breathing enough.
You might suffocate your friends trapped inside you.
Will you cry when the coroner extracts them from your body,
or did you cry long ago, knowing everything, perpetually hurting in advance?

The Incarnation

with a line from Linda Gregerson

Can you tell when the reed in the throat
                    has split?
            My infant girl coughs a cough as dogged

as the dregs of faith. Both keep me from my sleep,
                    awake,
            waiting for the next exhalation, blood

-shot eyes because this scratching in her lungs
                    has lasted seven days,
            this itch of doubt in my heart
                                        the entire year of her life.

The apostate's curse is to exhume
                    old habits
            when seeking mercy for others.

A catholicon for baby's throat,
                    pride and dignity the lavish amends.
            In the parlance of our time

I would say I am spiritual
                    but not religious,
            which has come to mean *I want a soul*

but not a body. I have no use for ears
                    having failed to divine the prime mover
            of my daughter's cold.
                                        I'm left with prayer,

the words of which I know by heart, the heat
                    of which is nothing more than neuron flame,
            holy ghost of synapse, the purple

scar from a hot oven rack, from the gray
                    ash of flung cigarette, from the shaking engine
box of my father's lawn mower.

I remember the prior week, back
        when her breath was the vapor of milk,
    as I do her ten months in utero,

as a time before I had all things to lose.
        But now the sonorous whoop
    fleecing her wind,

now the insomnia, now the heaven-spun hope
        that she might sleep.
    The revelation that I will not again
            close my eyes

until I am certain her chest will go on
        rising and falling,
    unable as I am to imagine a god

           to whom I might relinquish her body.

Xavier Viramontes, *Boycott Grapes, Support the United Farm Workers Union*, 1973, offset lithograph, Smithsonian American Art Museum, Gift of Tomás Ybarra-Frausto © 1973, Xavier Viramontes. Reproduced courtesy of Museum of Fine Arts, St. Petersburg, from "Our America: The Latino Presence in American Art."

Allison Campbell

What Work Is

Whenever I think about work, I hear poet Philip Levine's mixed-metal-like voice telling me I don't know what it is—"because you don't know what work is,"[1] says the last line of his poem—because I've never mistaken someone in line outside an auto-plant for my brother who sings Wagner when he's not at the factory. By this definition of the word, I don't know what work is. Though I do often mistake people for other people, and once spent hours scrubbing stainless steel ladders and handles at an indoor swimming pool. I was twenty, hungover, and the smell of the chemicals about did me in. Worst part was that after I scrubbed and scrubbed, the steel looked untouched, the white and green residue still imperfectly intact—like I hadn't tried to clean it. I was getting paid by the hour, so I kept going.

But back to Levine's steel. I associate his voice with metal for reasons of sound and sense. His tone is unbending, and he's able to make the simplest of words sound dense. He says, "Forget you" and I believe he means it, but keeps speaking to me anyway. In the recording, it's as though he threatens us with the poem's words and offers them as scaffolding. Sense-wise, the metal comes from knowing Levine grew up working in auto-plants. For me, auto-plants equal metal. Many metal machines working metal into other metal machines, with a few soft bodies scattered about and busy.

For a while, Levine was one of those bodies.

In "What Work Is" people are waiting, in the rain, for work. The poem's title sets you up for explanation, but inside it no one is *working*. And Levine never comes to a clear conclusion about what work is. In fact, the poem is purposely ambiguous—first he says "You know what work is— if you're / old enough to read this you know what / work is, although you may not do it." The concept being that one doesn't explain what one can only know by already knowing it. A very well-put "If I have to explain, you won't understand." You do or you don't. In the end, he switches to telling you "you don't know." The only conclusion to be made is that the speaker comes to no conclusion. Readers have to make up their own minds about work.

When Whitman wrote, "And there is no object so soft but it makes a hub for the wheel'd universe," I'm sure it was a precognitive nod to Detroit autoworkers.[2] This is fitting since Levine was dubbed "Whitman of the industrial heartland."[3] The Whitman moniker stems from Levine's ability to encompass many worlds inside his poems, but also, I believe, from Levine's hard brand of optimism. He writes about workers, Midwesterners, blue-collar people, without glorifying them—as Carl Sandburg is wont to do in *Chicago Poems*—or making them too morose—as Edgar Lee Masters does in his 1915 *Spoon River Anthology*, a book that comes to mind as supreme example of literature concerned with depressing Midwesterners.[4] Almost all of the characters

---

1. There is an excellent recording of Levine reading his poem "What Work Is" available through the podcast "Essential American Poets." But I also got to hear him read at Housing Works bookstore in New York. The recorded voice doesn't exaggerate; it is eerily consistent with the real thing—gruff but intense, a bit worn, and somehow incredibly hopeful.

2. Whitman published the first edition of *Leaves of Grass* in 1855. The Ford Highland Park plant Levine writes of

opened in 1910. It is now a National Historic Landmark.

3. Poet and critic Edward Hirsch bestowed the memorable description—"a large, ironic Whitman of the industrial heartland"—in his review of Levine's *Selected Poems* for the *New York Times*, August 5, 1984.

4. Admittedly, all the characters of *Spoon River Anthology* are speaking from the grave, where all that's left of life is reflection. Still, this reflection could be more balanced.

Masters writes of are extremely self-pitying. Being from the Midwest, and knowing a fair share of depressives, I admit there is some authenticity to the thwarted people he describes. The problem is, it's not the whole truth. Inside his poems, I find myself thinking *Oh, come on, it can't be that bad. Surely.* Maybe it was, though. Maybe my objections are generational, clouded by the plush version of working-class, middle-class Midwest I grew up in. I don't know. But in Levine's poems people can behave heroically without being heroes. There are depressing conditions, but people are not continually, or inevitably, depressed.

When I think about the times I've felt I was working—in the blue-collar, toiling kind of way, the way my father worked and Levine wrote about—I have always been hung-over and either outside in direct sunlight or some place with no air conditioning in July. Basically, suffering. Maybe this means I've psychologically linked work with suffering—I have, and it's probably because growing up I didn't know many people who liked their jobs. Levine was temporarily engaged in building automobiles; my father spent over thirty years repairing them. In both, there is the presence of parts, and putting them together to make a whole. Building and repairing seem akin to the production and revision processes of any creative art. My father enjoyed being a mechanic, solving engine puzzles and helping people in his way. But he had little, if any, respect for his boss. He didn't trust the dealership owner's intelligence, or decisions, and he didn't pretend otherwise. In return, the owner disliked my father. Still, my father kept this job, working for this man, for over twenty years. He liked his work.

The union is what kept the dealership owner's displeasure with my father from turning into unemployment. It kept him from being too much like the people waiting in "What Work Is," those in line with the "knowledge that somewhere ahead / a man is waiting who will say, 'No, / we're not hiring today,' for any / reason he wants." The boss made decisions my father disagreed with, for any reason he wanted, but taking away the job was one of the few things he could not do. All of this brings up issues of authority. In the poem, there is a man who has the authority to deny people the work they need to live. They can resent this predicament, or put up with it. Levine's workers endure. The speaker thinks he sees his brother, but it turns out to be "someone else's brother," who has "the same sad slouch, the grin / that does not hide the stubbornness, the sad refusal to give in" to the weather or the waiting. This man is a vulnerable, but not defeated, character. There's a certain way you are supposed to act toward authority, toward the man at the front of the line or your boss. Elements of kowtowing[5] exist with any work. My father was not overly skilled at this art of ingratiation and it made his work harder work, or made his work what might be better called a job.

This thinking about my father, and those waiting in Levine's poem, makes it seem that the problem with work is exclusively blue-collar. But disliking the authority of a boss seems a universal condition. Growing up, even my friends' fathers who wore suits were grumpy in the evening and guarded about their time on the weekends—as if at any moment someone could come up behind them while they were mowing the lawn or watching the game and yell "get back to work!" It didn't seem they loved their jobs either, but maybe—as my father did—they liked their work. I don't know. Seems the trick is to find work you enjoy and a job you can stand.

I started bussing tables at Patrick's Steakhouse in seventh grade, and moved up to waitressing in high school. One can make a lot of money in restaurants, picking up tips and in podunk places getting a bit of tax-free hourly under the table. I didn't like it. Not because the work was especially hard, but because I had to serve people and I wasn't that great at it.[6] Clearing one table I knocked over a water that splashed onto the

---

5. "Kowtow" comes from Chinese and literally means, "knock, head." This is funny because in English it's common to describe talking to a stubborn, unyielding person as "knocking your head against a wall"—the wall of the other person. I always thought of kowtowing as choice, but in the literal translation it is a forced necessity. Your head will rarely get its way against a wall.

6. Again, questions of authority. In the restaurant industry, every customer is temporarily your boss.

shorts of a man at the next. "I have to drive all the way back to _____ in these tonight!" he yelled. I apologized, but later repeated the line to myself as a joke. Didn't he have other pants he could wear? Underwear on? How could this be such a problem? Another time, I handed a blind woman a menu. How was I to know? Treating people equally, as I did. When she told me she was blind, I took the menu back in an awkward silence. Maybe I said I didn't know. I don't remember. But I remember she said, "You're supposed to say you're sorry." I didn't feel sorry and felt indignant about her telling me I should say so.

In fact, almost all memories of my restaurant years involve me feeling indignant about something. My boss asked if he was paying me to read and I asked which tables he could see that needed cleaning. When a customer complimented me on how well-spoken I was, I thanked him but thought, *why the hell not? Does being a waitress make this extraordinary?* Granted, these were my teenage years. I was indignant about a lot of things, in and outside of work, but what I quickly came to value about my next "profession" was that no one talked to me.

❖ ❖ ❖

With lifeguarding, you're usually too far away from people, usually sitting above them. And the posture assumed—a cross between being both alert and aloof (it would be creepy if you looked too interested)—does not encourage conversation. For years, I lifeguarded at my hometown pool and my undergraduate university's various aquatics facilities. My favorite of these jobs was at a practically abandoned boat dock on the university's campus. As one of the lifeguards there, I rented paddle-boats and canoes out on the small lake a professor of mine called "duck shit pond." I liked this job (despite the ducks and the shit, which there were, admittedly, more than enough of). Because up until this point, it was the least-like-work thing I'd ever gotten paid to do.

At the boat docks, we didn't have raised chairs, but we could avoid talking to people because they rarely visited. Paddle-boat rides were not popular with undergrads, and there were much better lakes, *real* lakes, in the area for people who were serious about canoeing. We did rent things

occasionally; a paddle-boat here and there to the random exchange student, group of stoners, or first-date couple. And Ponytail would come to windsurf. On days when there wasn't even a breeze, he'd come out with his thin, blond tail rubber-banded in increasingly smaller circles. We'd have to pull out the board and pole and sail from storage, then get his help rigging everything up. He'd sail off from the dock and we'd stand watching, hoping (from our worst portions) to see him fall. I'm not sure what annoyed us more, him making us get the equipment out or him never falling, whatever the weather. Seems to have been a competition between our laziness and schadenfreude, but not exactly. We wanted him to fall because he never fell, but also because he made us do what we did not want to do—work.

I write "we" because when I recall the boat docks I'm always with Bill. When we worked Saturdays together, he was usually drunk from Friday. Sometimes I was, too, probably, but more often I was hung-over and wondering why he had so much energy. The answer was Red Bull and vodka, which he drank like Gatorade. Once, while failing to get the BBQ going, he got frustrated and yelled, "We need more of this!" after which he chucked an empty, plastic liquor jug from one end of the pavilion (where he stood near the grill) to the other (where I stood near the boat dock office). On the usual Saturday this would have been okay, but it was Parents' Weekend, some of whom were walking up. I threw the bottle away and pretended I didn't hear him. *Don't mind the belligerent man at the grill, he doesn't work here.*

I could get paid for this. And most of the time it wasn't that chaotic. In nice weather, Bill and I would lie out on the dock and sun ourselves through long conversations about music (Bill was a DJ), art (Bill was also a painter), and recreational drugs (Bill had once gone temporarily blind while tripping and touring a Missouri cave). When we were in the sun, talking beautiful bullshit, I'd think *this is exactly what I should get paid to do.* There I was, making money, not hating it.

I didn't presume to think this was *work*, or that one could support himself or herself as a professional lifeguard in the Midwest. But if I could get paid to do this, the thinking went, what else might be out there. What other cakewalk things might someone earn a living at? Sky was the limit! I'd become an English major.

It wasn't only the boat docks that led to this degree; there was also modern dance and garbage bags. During my senior year of high school, I went to a performance where, in one piece, everyone—including my older sister—danced from inside garbage bags. They began on a dark stage, arranged in a circle on the floor. Imagine the face of a clock where the hour points are trash-bagged bodies. I see them starting entirely inside the bags, but they must have had their heads out. The dancers first used the plastic percussively, manipulating it from inside to create raspy patterns. I remember them rolling around inside the bags. Then arms and legs emerged, making each dancer a trash bag turtle. It was fantastic. Absurd and marvelous. Here my sister was studying dance, and someone was getting paid to choreograph this performance where the human body played with trash bags. Compared to this, becoming an English major seemed practical. On par with a nursing degree.

I think about telling my sister this story, explaining the performance's influence. But I'm not sure what it's worth as a compliment. I may sound like the well-meaning, diction-praising customer at the steakhouse. Why should I be surprised that modern dance inspires? But it's not only that. The feeling wasn't purely inspirational. I realized something pointless in the performance. It was the absurdity of Beckett (whom I hadn't read yet)—ostensibly fruitless, yet not futile. You could do something fruitless and just by it existing something about its fruitlessness was negated.[7] It seemed the opposite of work; anti-work.

The performance was play. It meant you could get paid—at least some people did—to play. This was important to see in contrast to another idea my father, who was also at the performance that evening, liked to repeat. His loosely defined category of *the real world*. It's written here in italics

because he would say this in italics. They were vocally italicized words that often popped into the conversation we were having and trumped whatever point I was trying to make. Throughout high school, when he used this phrase I thought he was referring to life outside of high school, outside our small town. "You know, *in the real world* . . . " he would say, or "*But in the real world.* . . . " The way he expressed this made me imagine a place one would be ushered into violently. One day I'd be driving my car, pass through a dense cloud, and coming out the other end everything would be much more *real*. And *real*, I thought, meant harder and more of a drag.

Then I went to college and started working at the boat docks. I took literature classes and drank myself into oblivions. Nothing seemed to get any more real. I actively tried to keep it from becoming so. Like the work in Levine's poem, the *real world* was never fully defined. Yet, somehow both work and the real world manage to be fully present, almost haunting forces. And, to me, the specter of my father's *real world* implied a place where personal truths were put into confrontation with external conditions (i.e. the importance of making art and necessity of eating) so violently that some reversal or revision of the personal was mandatory. I could catalogue here all the methods of avoidance I have used for the last decade or so—always fearing this real world's approach and finding some graduate school or foreign country, relationship or new city, to keep it at bay. But the time needed for this outweighs its entertainment value or importance. What is important, maybe, is that I'm still unconvinced this *real world* exists outside my father's imagination. If you asked him today, though, he might concede I'm there now; in my thirties, in a PhD program, with a child and the difficulties of attempting to stay married to someone. I don't know that I'd agree with his concession, because doing so would acknowledge the validity of the distinction. It would mean admitting that the real world—an outside force that cannot be ne-

---

7. I have always read Samuel Beckett's work as having an optimistic spirit, even when he's at his bleakest. Once, as a Valentine, I copied a section of one of his short stories where a man happens upon an abandoned cottage and finds, amongst other undesirable items, an arrowed heart traced and dried in cow manure. I thought it the most potent romantic comedy. The relationship went nowhere.

gotiated with—outmaneuvers any reality a person can work to create.

I do understand that when delineating between the real world and the place my father sensed me dreamily occupying, he was trying to impart some information he thought essential. The differentiation, however artificial, was supposed to instruct, be useful. Levine's poem makes a similar gesture. He's constantly addressing *you*. Telling you this standing, waiting, "feeling the light rain falling like mist," is work. Get it? This type of living is *real*, especially in contrast to what you, dear reader, dear daughter, know. But maybe I do know. Know enough to know I don't want to know more. I get tired. I am tired right now. My daughter has puked on me three times today, but do I have to suffer with it? With respect to Levine and my father, isn't it enough for me to experience it? To be up with her at four a.m. and writing now at eight?

In Elizabeth Bishop's poem "Questions of Travel" the speaker asks a similar but opposite question—"Oh, must we dream our dreams / and have them, too?" My version here is, must we have our troubles and suffer with them, too? Is this the only way to be real? What is most real about the brother in Levine's poem: the Cadillac he builds at night? The sleeping he does to recover? Or the Wagner he sings after he rises? Which is his work? Levine doesn't answer. I'm not sure I want to find out. Except, this is a lie. I do want to find out. If I'm honest, I see the small, ugly beast from Stephan Crane's "In the Desert" sneak out of my chest, squat on my shoulder, and causally snack on his own heart. "But I like it / Because it is bitter, And because it is my heart." He tells me, I do want to eat my heart out about my work, to fully know it. The difference lies in the *my* before work. When you start to identify as some sort of artist, the things you do become a *my* (*your* work). You want to get paid for this eventually, but this is second to (and lost in) the doing of the work. Work for a paycheck always comes with some authority, because there is someone doling out the checks. The dream is to do the work you want to do, and then have someone write the check. Working without knowledge of the check is what draws me to Crane's beast. In some ways, I know I am devouring myself, that

writing is a little like cannibalization. But better to eat your own heart, no matter the taste, than offer it up to someone else, right? To some boss or customer? Who doesn't want to use her own energy for her own aims? The other work, the type you're doing for someone else, I don't want to know. This is one of the reasons that, when younger, I never wanted to become a teacher. I was never that interested in what I saw then as self-sacrifice.

But sometimes we become things we don't mean to become. That's the way it has been with me, at least. After undergrad, I went to graduate school for creative writing. Then, not sold on the idea of more academia, going on to get my PhD, or moving to New York to make a go of it in publishing, I decided to teach in Japan. I wanted to live and write. I wanted to be a writer, without making something else of myself. But I needed to eat. Teaching abroad seemed the perfect stopgap.

I was a floating teacher in a junior high school in Ashikaga City. I went to each English class once a week and assisted with pronunciation exercises. This gig is ideal for someone who wants to get paid to teach but not become attached to teaching in a way that could distract her from her *real* work, writing. I didn't know most of the kids' names, I couldn't pronounce many of their names, and I didn't try. I liked them, I talked to them, we played games, sang songs, took quizzes—but that was it. I couldn't understand any of the school speeches, and the kids' English wasn't advanced enough for in-depth conversation.[8] Everything was light, on the surface, and I found it easy to pretend at any emotion necessary for the job (which, in general, was a mixture of profound gratitude and controlled excitement; all the Japanese went in for this. As long as you didn't show any extreme emotions and avoided sickness and injury, you were golden).

But teaching in Japan wasn't all show. What happened in Ashikaga was that one school term ended and the next began. A new batch of kids came from the elementary school, and they looked so damned elementary—collections of miniature parts that could someday be assembled

---

8. Mostly, we talked ice-cream flavors and favorite pets.

into full people. They seemed too small for the desks and stairwells, they had gooey-watery eyes like the cartoon dogs with oversized heads, and almost all of them were terribly shy. Mostly, they giggled. And there were two with disabilities. The first was almost blind. He had a large magnification device upon and overtaking his desk; this sight, combined with his diligence, was a little too much.[9] The second, Kioshi, was obsessive-compulsive. He had a bald stripe running across the center of his head, about two-finger-widths thick, stretching from forehead to crown. He maintained this patch by pulling hairs from his head during class and eating them. He did not talk or smile. He was not doughy-eyed. And I was scared of him. He was so small but so stern, so unapproachable. I taught him for months without hearing anything, neither English nor Japanese. Like all the students I taught, I really knew nothing of his interior (his home life, personality, or hopes). The difference with him was that instead of putting up, or even possessing, some veneer for me to work with, he was putting something of the inside out. This kid pretended nothing. And you didn't need to speak a certain language to read the stripe across his head.

The Japanese have these clear and long-sided umbrellas that you are more inside than under. You can look through them, but every thing is a bit blurry. I was walking home from school in one. There was a light rain and I remember the drops on my umbrella obscuring the landscape. At some point, I became aware that Kioshi was beside me on the road. I didn't hear or see him approach, had never seen him walk this way after school. Between the rice fields and rain, his school uniform and my umbrella, this seemed like the perfect opening scene of some Japanese horror-film. I half-expected to see a pair of school scissors in his hand. For a moment, I thought about returning with him to the junior high and handing him over to some Japanese-speaking teacher, telling myself that it was to make sure *he* would get home safely.

But the kid interrupted my anxieties by reaching a hand outside his umbrella and saying "rain." Then he smiled at me like he had made the most

fantastic joke. A bit Helen-Keller-at-the-water-spigot, but this is what happened. Suddenly, Kioshi was speaking English. It was barely raining now, so we both took down our umbrellas and let the random drops hit us, said "rain" a few more times. We continued walking and he pointed out other objects and colors. Sky, grass, water, blue, bird, road. After each word he'd look at me, like we were conspirators, like these words were great secrets he was glad to let me in on. And they were—before that walk all the words he knew were his own secrets—possibly even secret to himself. Did he know he knew them before that afternoon? I like to believe that he might not have known, because it makes the discovery more shared. But this most likely romanticizes things. He probably knew what he knew—the smiles definitely hinted at this. Ultimately, there's no way to tell. What I do know is, after we parted, I walked back to my apartment feeling wonderful, feeling like (although I wouldn't name it in this way) something *real* had happened.

It wasn't until I stopped walking, till I arrived, that the dread set in. The thought, *that kid just turned me into a teacher*, was chased by, *I don't want to be teacher*. I quickly decided I still didn't have to be, I could let the encounter go, a nice little event. It didn't need to be life changing. Every experience was not the universe granting me permission to exist, calling me to account for my presence, or instructing me on how to live. But I knew something had changed during the walk. This kid showed me there were a lot of inner workings about which I was clueless. Someone could take something I said and secretly spin it around in whatever dark resources he or she possessed. I would most likely never know the terminus of these processes—and they weren't mine to know.

I wasn't thinking of all of this with Kioshi, I just realized the kid made me like something I did not want to like (teaching), made me care about something I did not want to care about (him). He complicated my idea of working at the junior high. It was supposed to be a job, a job that would give me enough money to live and leave me enough time to write—I wasn't interested in a *Mr. Holland's Opus* scenario—and at the time I thought this encounter threatened the deal. Now I can see the threat I felt was very

---

9. By "too much" I mean exactly enough to make even an actively distancing person sentimental.

Poet Philip Levine at the 75th Anniversary of the Iowa Writers Workshop in June 2011. Photo by Carmen Maria Machado.

much like my father's *real world*, a false division of my own making. In the end, everything we do is work and there is only one world. I can drop the pretentious *my* prefix and get on with it. I am willing to be less of an artist if it helps me live in this one place where we work and dream, boss and yield, daily. A friend once told me he was making his life into a "work of art." At the time, I thought this both grandiose and lazy. He had just married an opera singer and was honeymooning in Rome. I remember thinking *Okay, so now you're done*. How did he expect to be so great without making anything but himself? Now I think, yeah, why the hell not? The idea that I may be my own best work makes me a whole lot less afraid of everything I do between here and the hereafter. When, as it is now with Levine, my work is done.[10]

❖ ❖ ❖

10. Philip Levine died on February 14th, 2015. I began writing this essay the morning of his death, not knowing that he had died until that afternoon. My friend Rodney Jones says it best: "No poet brought such a keen balance of gravitas and levity as Philip Levine. As if, at any instance, he needed to channel John Keats and both Karl and Groucho Marx to be his whole self. And this was true of both his poems and his person. A dear, ferocious, and compassionate man, he gave what we need still and so rarely find. Poetry."

An Old Story

The trouble was, Luise said,
he was *strikingly Jewish-looking . . . loud . . .*
I stumbled on this in a book . . . My grandfather
waving his arms and saying—what?—
on the train to Switzerland. His arrest
at Singen. My grandmother *pale with terror.*
But I see her faking smiles and warmth
in her light blue eyes to slip by guards,
crawling that night across the border,
while he, whom she'd never see again,
went east. Luise Meier was the one
she blamed . . . Or so it says.

Again and again, this book, these fragments,
sieved for gold. Luise Meier,
saving almost thirty Jews,
my grandfather *not* betraying his helpers.
But what was said on the train? What's lost
to silence, in bitter or wishful retelling?
I think of cooling lovers, the scorn
with which they wrench themselves apart,
how quickly we transform our saviors,
loved ones, lost ones into demons,
or into icons, trapped forever
in their final, terrible moments.

Ditch-dirt, ash, a plume of smoke,
this train is roaring through my blood,
crammed with shattered lives, sometimes
distant, barely heard, sometimes
screeching closer. I hold on tight
to this quiet room, the lamps, the books,
the sleeping cats, and through the window
the large moon, still there, still there.

Lance Larsen

Aphorisms for a Lonely Planet

Journeys begin not with a first step, but with a door left ajar. The moon, that old megaphone—she sings by whispering. Envy the young their ignorance, not their perfect bodies. Carry a violin in your trunk only if you're willing to rosin up. A haiku a day keeps the epic away. Add white to your gazebo by lining the path with deer skulls. If it can hop, it has a soul. Most serious sins involve the tongue. Like the Chinese, dress your young daughter in rat shoes so that Death will pass her by. Crack open windows to encourage airflow and surprise visits from heretofore invisible gods. Never lecture a dust storm. Neglect not the slippery wisdom of a bar of soap. Stir clockwise, think counterclockwise. Dead lovers live on in the rivers of your wrist. From far enough away all disasters resemble spring weather. It takes two to carry an effigy of yourself to the top of the hill, but only one to toss the match.

Lance Larsen

A Little Blood on the Ceiling

A violent faded spray of it, in the maternity ward at St. Joseph's, room 331, a swath of it, or was it a path? I was a new father on a cot, and this was a ten-foot ceiling. You do the physics. Whose blood? I had no idea. Maybe an orderly got shot, maybe some weirdo witch doctor was swinging a bleeding cat by its tail, that kind of splatter pattern and palimpsest. And I was trying to doze off to the oceany whoosh of machines, and my newborn was pure mouth, and my sutured beloved was all breast, and both were sleeping off this new hunger. How does blood swim out of the body like that? Aren't there laws of gravity? I've seen fast blood, warm sloshing blood, life-in-turmoil blood, we're-going-to-need-a-transfusion blood, but not blood-on-the-ceiling blood. Milk should have been the only currency of exchange that night, first colostrum, later the foremilk and hindmilk, yes the rich creamy stuff stuffed with antibodies and tomorrows and all contracts maternal. Bring me a ladder, I thought, and soap, and I'll clean up this ancient stain. A ladder that unfolds like a metallic praying mantis, like God himself—make it sturdy and aluminum so He won't rust in Houston rain. And I'll put on steel-toed boots, or squeeze into nurse shoes, hell I'll climb bare foot if needs be. I have good arms and agility and know how to scrub. Maybe so, said that mystery blood to my blood, but there will be other stains no ladder can reach. When I closed my eyes, I felt myself drifting in circles, a skiff under a pink moon.

Lance Larsen

Valentine Poem Written After a Tragic Mishap in Local Cave

I love you like wanderlust, like the idiot spelunker jonesing for something twisty and unmapped and forever. Which he got. And voyeuristic media coverage to boot: no backing up inside that widow maker. The more he panicked the tighter he wedged himself. I love you like his two buddies who couldn't pull him free, not with ropes or straps or prayer. And like the county rescue team using oils domestic and lubricants industrial, not to mention a portable winch, which also failed, breaking ribs and almost snapping his neck. Twelve, nineteen, thirty-four: local reporters tracked every stuck hour, and still he swelled. And now I love you with whatever heroics it took to keep him comfortable. The mountain pressing down is our time on this planet, love. What we breathe in, everything else. I don't need extra flashlight batteries to remember your body. I love you like a mole rat making a nest of chewed hemp, like Tic Tacs crushed in a spelunker's pocket. Is it true they'll spark up a bed after canoodling? Shall we turn down the lights? If I, like the drip of cave water getting to the bottom of things? If you, like plastic flowers laid at the cave's mouth? If I with the afterlife thrumming in my toes, if you carrying the weight of Portland cement? Thirty-seven sloppy wheel-barrows of the stuff—that's what it took the Army Corps of Engineers to seal the entrance and convert cave into grave. I love you like robins warbling, a broken stanza of them too spent to fly south, like tire tracks re-freezing twice since Sunday. You be Indian paintbrush come May. I'll be the sunflower seeds you crack one at a time to make sadness last.

Suzanne Williamson. *A View of the Temple Mound Overlooking the Crystal River: Crystal River Archaelogical State Park, Citrus County, Florida.* Framed photographic print. 48 x 48 inches. Copyright © Suzanne Williamson 2009.

Thomas Hallock

Into the Swamp

In 1984 a pair of young archaeologists, graduate students at the time, rediscovered a low-slung, twenty-foot midden called Tatham Mound, not far from central Florida's Withlacoochee River. Tucked into a dense stand of scrub oak, the mound yielded harrowing evidence of a 1539 encounter between soldiers in Hernando De Soto's army and Gulf Coast Indians. The archeologists found skeletons reportedly hacked by steel weapons, bodies buried with plates of Spanish brigantine, or armor, and chevron-shaped (six-sided) glass beads directly traceable to other sites along the Spaniards' four-year path.

We cannot help but read into funereal mounds; the legacies of conquest lend archaeology a moral weight, and the discoveries at Tatham all but cried for interpretation. The first studies argued that an epidemic must have followed the Spanish invasion of *la Florida*. Below the strata with evidence of contact on Tatham Mound, from 1539, bodies had been lain in neat rows; above them, the bones were scattered akimbo, like the mass grave of a collapsed society. The Spaniards took some lives with their swords, in other words, but far more with pathogens. Subsequent researchers have been slower to attach meaning to the bones, however. Providing a much-needed alternative to the catastrophe-hypothesis, bioarchaeologist Dale L. Hutchinson concedes that the population along Florida's Gulf Coast fell in the sixteenth century—although probably because the Indians left, avoiding further conflicts with the Spanish. Disease hit later, after migration and social change had weakened native resistances. And anthropologist Brent Weisman, the first to dig at Tatham Mound, gives an entirely undramatic reason for the chipped bones. He said (to students anyway) that he accidentally chipped some skeletons with the blade of his shovel, a major "no-no," but not uncommon in the early stages of an excavation.

When we dig up bones, we dig up stories. Presented with the new evidence from Tatham Mound, Weisman's former advisor, an energetic and enormously creative scholar named Jerald Milanich, linked forensics to the narrative record. Dialing up the most accurate of the expedition's four primary texts, Rodrigo Ranjel's *Account of the Northern Conquest and Discovery of Hernando de Soto*, Milanich pegged the hacked skeletons to this particular passage:

> The Indians, on two occasions, killed three soldiers of the guard of the Governor and wounded others and killed a horse, and all that was done to poor order since those Indians, although they are archers and have very strong bows and are very skillful and accurate marksmen, their arrows do not have poison [*hierba*] nor do they know what it is.

The link between textual and material evidence allowed scholars to reconstruct the first year of De Soto's campaign. The Indians who fought the Spanish guards, presumably, were interred along the Withlachoochee. Starting from Tatham Mound, scholars could move backwards and forwards, from the entrada at Tampa Bay (some had thought Charlotte Harbor to the south) to the army's winter encampment outside present-day Tallahassee.

The familiar name, Hernando De Soto, would also serve as a grant-writing bonanza. Taking the scholarship public, university researchers lobbied vigorously for a state-wide De Soto Trail, which they hoped would pilot a federally-funded trail—a Southern equivalent to the Lewis and Clark phenomenon. Their efforts proved successful (Hernando De Soto inadvertently funded a decade of semi-related projects, from Franciscan missions to a history of the Seminoles) and the Florida De Soto Trail launched in 1985, complete with pamphlet maps, signage, and a series of eleven interpretative kiosks that narrated the brutal encounter from Inverness to the Georgia line. Governor Bob Graham attended the first kiosk's dedication, off Highway 41 (as close as one can get to Tatham Mound without a swamp buggy), and the unveiling featured the usual mix of scholarly assurance and theatrical flair. The Crystal River High School band opened with the national anthem. A corseted Queen Isabella and bare-chested Timucuan Indians stood to the side through the entire ceremony. Then the erudite Graham, a Harvard-trained attorney and future presidential candidate, pulled the brown cloth from the tile-roofed display. Despite the initial enthusiasm, however, the Conquistadors failed to generate the same patriotic fervor as Lewis and Clark. Interest flagged. The federally funded National Parks Service trail never materialized, scholars prevaricated on the route, and Florida's backroad markers—intended as the portals for deeper historical understanding—served as target practice for passing motorists.

My wife, Julie, first noticed the De Soto Trail not long after we married and moved South, in the mid-nineties. At the time she was researching a novel set in north Florida. The novel never materialized, but the narratives caught my interest as an Early Americanist, and over the next few years, we re-traced the scholarly and touristic routes. Armed with the definitive academic study, Milanich and Charles Hudson's *Hernando de Soto and the Indians of Florida*, we soon accumulated a carton full of Conquistador kitsch and an affection for the quirky backwaters of our adopted home state. William Least Heat-Moon's classic *Blue Highways* was still in vogue, and the trail from Bradenton (home to the National Park Service's "De Soto Landing Memorial") to Tallahassee took us off the Disney route, down older and more resonant roads—Highways 41 and 301, historic north-south arteries, and US-90, an old Indian trace that parallels the Interstate through courthouse towns across the Panhandle. Along the way we discovered a lost Florida of dogtrot houses; "Born Again Used Cars" in Groveland; points on the Suwannee where the river was forded (where it is wider and more shallow) rather than bridged; a Florida of groveside orange stands, local produce and honey, Confederate flags, and country girls in bikini tops, mowing the yard on miniature John Deeres.

In a state defined by reinvention, by Spring Break and theme parks, we discovered what archaeologists call time-depth, places like the Cove of the Withlacoochee, a border region that encapsulates three centuries of Florida history, where Tatham Mound still lies. A Seminole name, Withlacoochee means "little big water." The name is apt. Wide, shallow lakes on the 150-mile Withlacoochee River dilate into shallow streams not ten feet across; water levels fluctuate wildly with the seasons. This spring-fed, black-water river is a living oxymoron, a study in liminality (Latin word, not related to the Greek *limn*, pertaining to lakes). For precontact groups, the Cove of the Withlacoochee marked the boundary between coastal Safety Harbor people and the agricultural Timucuans to the North. Colonial disruptions had emptied the landscape by the eighteenth century, but by this point, the maze of swamps and middens would serve as a retreat for free blacks, escaping British slave colonies to the north. These maroons assimilated with the Seminoles, who waged a costly war with the United States through the first half of the nineteenth century. The famed Osceola (née Billy Powell) made camp at Powells Town, not far from a maroon community and Tatham Mound, which he valued for both tactical and ceremonial reasons. Today the swampy Cove of the Withlacoochee is protected by Wildlife Management Areas; it is a gap in the USGS grid, with a small tourist draw for airboat rides, but used mostly for hunting and fishing. The graduate students who rediscovered Tatham Mound relied upon local knowledge (a renowned turkey hunter in the area), plus a map by a West Pointer named Henry Prince, who documented the chase for Osceola during the Second Seminole War in a topographically-rich journal. With military precision, Prince detailed the contours of a deep-time landscape that connected Florida's late precontact era, the long history of slavery in British America and the United States, and a series of wars still never closed with a formal treaty of peace.

Having circled fruitlessly around De Soto narratives for years, I wanted to cross the Cove of the Withlacoochee myself. So I custom-ordered a topo map from a GPS company based out of Billings, Montana, (store-bought maps split the

Cove into two grids) and consulted with the husband of a former student, a professional archeologist who works out of an office park near the Tampa airport. My friend rendered for me a pdf map of the protected sites—including Powell's Town, the maroon community (on a hammock called Kettle Island), and Tatham Mound.

I asked if he wanted to cruise the swamp with Julie and me. "I don't know," he laughed, "you gotta be pretty packed with desire to go there." I was nothing if not packed with desire. I pieced together an itinerary. We would park by an outlet stream of the With, just south of Lake Panasoffkee. We would paddle to Panasoffkee, cross the seasonally flooded Princess Lake, then enter Tsala Apopka, a body of water that skirts Kettle Island. From the old maroon settlement there, if my map was correct, we should find a channel to Powell's Town, where we could camp and find a jeep trail to Tatham Mound.

❖ ❖ ❖

Julie and I launched on Sunday morning, a few weeks later, not long before Easter. We parked at a county park below Lake Panasoffkee, loaded up our red Old Town, and let the spring-fed outlet stream carry us into the swampy Cove. Buzzards climbed the thermals. Spotted gar nosed against the current, suspended in the crystalline water, as if by magic, above the pocked limestone river bed. A belted kingfisher darted bank to bank. Precontact Indians etched the profile of these squat, angular birds onto funereal pots. Milanich maintains that the boundary-crossing kingfisher served as a guide in the journey after death; kingfishers fly through the air, frequent rivers, and nest in the earth, making them the perfect embodiment of a liminal state. I made a mental note, remembering that the kingfisher also serves as a halcyon symbol in Virgil's *Georgics*.

Elemental boundaries dissolve on the Little Big Water. Hunters shoot from skiffs; hikers wade. The outlet stream off Panasoffkee would feed into Tsala Apopka, although the lake was now prairie, and because it was early Spring, nesting season for female alligators, Julie would not let me stand in the canoe to peek over the grass. We edged near Kettle Island. According to my topo map, we should see the hammock that was

Powell's Town on the right. But the current had shot us past our landmark; we were lost, and by this point, had not stepped foot on solid ground for several hours. The slapping black water set us both on edge. Julie was premenstrual.

Over the course of a marriage, a couple will work out some strategies for settling their differences. Julie and I talk best over food. So I steered our Old Town to a stand of cypress. After a brief scare—an alligator guarding the shady spot where we hoped to eat—I wedged the canoe between two cypress knees. We snacked on carrots, pita and hummus. A truism among critics in my secondary academic field, nature writing, is that we can read our way into a written text. If the environmental plays an active role in a literary work, the thinking goes, then narrative scholarship (a combination of storytelling and traditional research) should yield meaning. I follow models like Ian Marshall, who hikes through the literature of the Appalachian Trail, and John Elder, a Robert Frost expert who taught for decades at Middlebury and Bread Loaf. Elder writes that "the mountains may also be carried along in a hiker's rucksack, in company with a water bottle and topo map." Nudged between cypress knees, easily mistaken for half-submerged gator heads, Elder's language feels a bit trite. (Who actually uses the word "rucksack" anyway?) Topographical maps work in the mountains, but in the Little Big Water, where the lines marking green and blue fluctuate with the seasons, the map is no more reliable than the literature.

Julie and I struck a bargain—a compromise. With enough time to backtrack to Panasoffkee, we could grab a motel room in Inverness, order a pizza, and mark this trip as yet one more failed attempt at Thoreauvian contact. We agreed to paddle another thirty minutes, and if we did not find solid ground, we would turn around. So I packed our leftovers back in the cooler and pushed against a cypress knee. We turned a river bend. Then a miracle. A hardwood hammock, a quarter-mile ahead, with an airboat banked on a half-crumbled concrete ramp. I pointed the bow left, outside the main channel and into a thick mat of hydrilla, an invasive that clogs Florida's eutrophied rivers and lakes. Thick ropes of vegetation tangled around our canoe paddles, sapping the strength from our already dead shoulders. Desperation tugged us forward. We dug deep and reached the landing before the airboat left. I pulled our Old Town onto the ramp.

The airboaters, locals, helped us find our spot on the map, then disappeared back into the swamp, leaving a cyclone of smoke and noise in their wake, and the two of us to our unmarked campsite. I pitched our tent in a grove of live oak and sour orange trees, then gathered ground wood for a fire. Julie heated up our dinner of pasta and pesto. After supper, we settled by the banked fire with our journals and a bottle of wine, watching the darkness fall on our accidental wilderness. A full moon cast dappled shadows through the moss-draped live oak. Just before dusk, a pair of barred owls swooped above us and perched by the canoe. Working between my journal, the topo map, and my pdf of protected sites, I pieced together our location in time and space. Most likely, we had wound up on Kettle Island, the old maroon community. Writing in 1837, Lieutenant Henry Prince said Powell's Town was "a hiding place but little known even amongst the Indians." Literary geography had taken me to an obvious realization: that Osceola and the escaped slaves knew where to hide.

So what did I expect to accomplish here? Would I sip black drink with Billy Powell? Trade confidences with the skeleton holding a plate of brigantine? Historical scholarship on De Soto puts a premium on location, on accuracy and reliability, for good reason. The trails followed by De Soto's army led somewhere; they connected villages, so through the wanderings of a sixteenth-century conquistador, we get a rare snapshot of the precontact South. But the grounding in place, the fixation with narrative accounts that say little more than *De Soto was here*, can also leave us bereft. They say so little.

Three first-hand narratives of the 1539-43 expedition survive: Ranjel's *Account*; an account for the king prepared by Luys Hernandez de Biedma; and a *Relaçom Verdadeira* by the unnamed "Fidalgo," or Gentleman of Elvas. These three narratives anchor the historical and public scholarship, including the former kiosk along Highway 41 back in Inverness. A fourth narra-

Julie Armstrong and Thomas Hallock rest at the edge of the swamp.

tive, meanwhile, syncretic and not by a participant-observer, has never quite found its footing among place-haunted historians: *La Florida*, by El Inca Garcilaso de la Vega. This 1601 book, the first published by a Native American about a subject in the future United States, is a case study in neglect. Equal parts chivalric romance and morality tale, *La Florida del Inca* focuses less on day-to-day events than on the heroic qualities of the encounter—from both sides, Spanish *and* indigenous. Unlike Ranjel, who moves in one direction, El Inca Garcilaso switches back and forth, bridging cultural divides as he also planes across barriers of time. With the Inca, readers get more of the story than *just passing through.*

Consider the biography. The once-and-future author was born Gomez Suarez de Figueroa in Cuzco, Peru, in 1539 (the year De Soto touched ground off Tampa Bay). His father, Sebastian Garcilaso de la Vega, served Francisco Pizarro as a captain in the invasion of Peru; his mother, Chimpu Ocllu, witnessed the Inca's fall. Educated at the Cuzco cathedral, the illegitimate son journeyed to Spain in his early twenties, where he lived most of his life, and where he was promptly schooled in the power of colonial reportage. According to Francisco Lopez de Gomara's *Historia general de las Indias y conquista de Mexico* (1552), his father (Sebastian Garcilaso) had rebelled against Francisco Pizarro during the Peruvian campaign. This minor note in Gomora proved damning. While petitioning for a patrimony before the Royal Council of the Indies, the son was asked: "Historians have recorded this [rebellion], do you deny it?" The future author lost his case. In Peru's Biblioteca Nacional, or National Library, there is a copy of Gomara's *Historia general* with a marginal note in the hand of El Inca Garcilaso: "*Esta mentira me had quitado el comer quicas por mejor*"—this lie has prevented me from eating well.

The failed petition would shape the future book. (We are now some distance from a swamp in Gulf central Florida. But not really.) Scholarly consensus holds that the seeds for *La Florida* were sown in the halls of the Council of the Indies, where the future author met a veteran of the De Soto expedition named Gonzalo Silvestre—a retired captain who was also seeking a petition, and who would play a disproportionately large role in the published account. *La Florida* took shape from there, with layers building to give the book deeper resonance. The first mention of a De Soto history appeared in a 1590 translation by the author of *Dialogos de Amor*, by Léon Hebreo, and if we are to take Garcilaso at his word, he would consult other sources. The published *La Florida del Inca* cites some lost "Peregrinaciones" (or wanderings) by Alonso de Carmona, plus a tattered manuscript "half eaten by rats" by the foot soldier Juan Coles, supposedly discovered in a Cordoban bookshop. Did the Carmona and Coles texts ever exist—or was the author playing the favorite literary trick of "found papers?" Who knows? The point is that *La Florida del Inca* evolved in a recursive manner, from 1561 to a final form in 1601, and the extended composition would result in a work that reflects back and forth, in a dizzying series of doublings, upon the tenuous place of the Americas—and indigenous people especially—in the Spanish-speaking world.

La Florida del Inca starts from a place of difference, marking the story from a world apart. In the book's opening "Proemio," the narrator establishes a balance between distance and immediacy, objective fact and rhetorical persuasion. On one hand, he defines his role as "scribe" and "amanuensis," who reports on his sources "verbatim"; on the other hand, he announces his own rhetorical ends, "to acquire and populate this kingdom and convert its native population." Straddling this paradox, between unvarnished truth and persuasion, is the one holding the mirror—the historian himself—El Inca Garcilaso. *La Florida del Inca* recounts *his* Florida; if he has erred, then "*porque soy Indio*"—it is because he is an Indian. Enrique Pupo-Walker, one of the author's most incisive critics, describes an "individualized space of narration," a half-imagined and contradictory realm that can accommodate both objective and subjective fact. No single history coheres; we have instead a textual rupture, to use a favorite postcolonial term, in this attempt to bridge physical and narrative planes. While rhetorically spanning an ocean, the historian El Inca Garcilaso synthesizes a sometimes varied account that points to slips in translation—that acknowledges an American on the other side of the ocean, facts over there, *por allá.*

Translation, not surprisingly, looms large in *La Florida del Inca*. The author focuses on Juan Ortiz, an Andalucian who was stranded during Pánfilo de Narváez's 1528 landing off Tampa Bay, retrieved by De Soto a decade later. Juan Ortiz performed an invaluable service to De Soto as translator, and given his intermediary status, El Inca Garcilaso used him as a figure to explicate his own rhetorical dilemma. When first discovered by the Spanish soldier Alvaro Nieto, the castaway was said to cry "Xivilla, Xivilla," by which the historian explains, "he intended to say 'Sevilla, Sevilla.'" After a decade amongst the Indians, Ortiz had forgotten Spanish, so he would make "a sign of the cross with his hand and his bow so that his opponent may recognize him as a Christian." Words fail, prompting a long explanation about the author's own struggles remembering his native Quechua:

> . . . having found no person in Spain with whom I may speak my mother tongue, which is the one generally used in Peru (although the Incas have a special language that they employ in speaking among themselves), I have forgotten it that I cannot construe a sentence of as many as six or seven words which will convey my meaning, and I cannot remember many of the Indian terms necessary to name such and such an object. . . . Thus I have found through experience that one learns the words of a strange language by using them, but that he likewise forgets those of his own language by failing to use them.

Anyone who has struggled with a second language will recognize this key point, *use it or lose it*. But the narrator's unique position, more directly to the point, underscores the problems of settling this work on a specific location. The terrain of *La Florida del Inca* shuttles from North America to the Andes to the Iberian Peninsula.

Small wonder that historians of the expedition, linking text and bones, are all thumbs with El Inca Garcilaso. *La Florida del Inca* is ranked the least reliable of the four De Soto narratives. But the three other sources, moving in one direction, pose a far more significant problem. They make no attempt to negotiate a cultural divide. Rodrigo Ranjel's *Account*, an anchor of route scholarship, spools events down the road with a string of temporal signposts and conjunctions. We get: "the next day," or "as the sun was setting" and

"without losing time." The syntax of a chronicle hurls events into the next frame:

> And as the Christians ran forth against them, the Indians, fleeing, plunged into a forest, and one of them came forth to the road, saying, "Sirs, for the love of God and of St. Mary do not kill me: I am Christian, like you, and I am a native of Seville, and my name is Juan Ortiz."

Where Ranjel faces the constraints of genre, he can only move forward. *La Florida del Inca* has time on its side. Being a work of history (rather than the daily chronicle) the book may toggle between present, past and future—allowing it also to range across space, from Florida, to the author's Incan homeland, and back to the Spanish court.

Time fleshes out the consequences. With literature (unlike archeology) the skeletons get a chance to speak. From a tactical and historical perspective, Juan Ortiz bridged the 1528 landing of Pánfilo de Narváez and De Soto's 1539 arrival at Tampa Bay. The genre of a Renaissance history would allow the narrative space needed to fill in those intervening years. In a twist of the later Pocahontas narrative, *La Florida del Inca* would open with the meeting of Narváez and Chief Hirrihigua. The Spaniards kill the cacique's mother and cut off his nose. El Inca Garcilaso plots these events to establish a plausible series of occurrences. Hirrihigua tortures Juan Ortiz, and Ortiz is almost killed in retaliation, but he is rescued by our Princess Hirrihigua. Juan Ortiz then flies to a rival cacique, Mucozo, who is holding *Sevillano* captive when De Soto's army enters the scene in 1539.

The stuff of fiction provides the grounding for a story set far-off. Motives ground actions. Even though he describes an unfamiliar place, a Florida he had seen over a ship's prow at best, El Inca Garcilaso worked a position from the middle that would allow him to bridge cultural—and temporal—divides. His Indians act rationally; Hirrihigua's present is a product of the past. "When Pamphilo de Narvaez had gone to conquer the province," the historian explains, "he had waged war with Hirrihigua and later he had converted the Indian to friendship; then for some unknown reason, he had committed certain abuses against the Cacique which are of too odious a nature to be told here." But what was "too odious to be told"? Two chapters earlier, readers had learned that Narváez had killed the cacique's mother and cut off his nose. "Outrage knows no forgiveness," as El Inca Garcilaso explains the retaliation:

> . . . each time that Hirrihigua recalled [how] the Spaniards had cast his mother to the dogs and permitted them to feed upon her body, and each time that he attempted to blow his nose and failed to find it, the Devil seized him with the thought of avenging himself on Juan Ortiz, as if that young man had deprived him of his nostrils.

With colonial violence for a birthright, El Inca Garcilaso would provide a counternarrative to the encounter. *La Florida del Inca* offers a backstory, contrasting to the scribbling conquistadors tolling off the lists of hostages taken, towns passed, murders and dismemberment. And so we have a story from the swamp. Even as *La Florida del Inca* drifts without apology from its nominal subject to courtly romance, his book speaks a truth from Tatham Mound. What else can we say about the bones nicked by steel weapons—or a shovel? Without him we have little besides DNA evidence, a flat meditation on poison arrows, chevron-shaped beads, plates of rusted armor and dirt.

Thomas Hallock is ready to hit the trail.

❖ ❖ ❖

Julie and I broke camp in the hardwood hammock, reloaded our canoe, and threaded the thin channel we had cut through the hydrilla the previous evening. I set the creased topo map on our cooler and let the current pull us down this dirty rug of a river. Our view widened at Tsala Apopka, now prairie though a large blue splotch on the map from Billings, Montana. Along the edge of the hammock, probably near Kettle Island, two locals had banked an airboat. I spied a break in the hardwoods to our left, what I assumed to be Powell's Town. We debated our dilemma. The branch to our left was too low to paddle, the shore too muddy to walk; the swamp was full of gators. Buoyed by a fresh night's sleep and the promise of a metaphor, we poled our way through the muck. Ten minutes of grueling work took us a hundred yards closer. A guy on the airboat answered a cellphone call; his voice carried across the lake, "I'm sober now, bro." Buzzards circled above us. I considered the wake a hungover airboater might leave. We turned around, Julie now paddling stern and me in front, retracing the thin black sheen we had cut through the muck. We were back at Panasoffkee in time for lunch.

Two years passed. Julie and I would brave one last search for Tatham Mound. Actually planning this time, I filed for a backwoods permit. The outdoor rec coordinator at our school lent me his GPS, an already outdated model with an LED screen. On the drive to Inverness, I punched in the coordinates to our campsite and the protected sites. I planned a hike in from the west, tracing the edge of Flying Eagle Wildlife Management District, down a relic dune. We could camp at an equestrian site along Moccasin Slough, then follow a jeep trail to Dike Road, the western border of the WMA. From there, my topo map showed a second trail veering off the dike road, toward Tatham Mound.

We parked by the horse gate, shouldered our packs, and trekked towards Moccasin Slough. Following a slight downhill, we made good time. My topo map, printed on cheap paper and now several years old, was falling apart; before this trip I stuck together the pieces with archival tape. We followed electronic breadcrumbs on the GPS towards the permitted campsite. But this trail was off the backpackers' usual path. With less than an hour of daylight, the blazes started to disappear. We could not find our camp. Thinking a filter alone would be fine in a swamp, I had packed just two bottles of water. The only spot to refill was an algae-covered sink. Julie fretted over how we would boil our pasta. The Dike Road ran across the grass prairie, then through a series of higher hardwood hammocks, before unbraiding into a tangle of rabbit trails. We walked twenty minutes past the last blaze, still no campsite, and abandoned our plan. We pitched a dry camp in the dark. An airboat gunned in the distance but we saw no sign of water. I improvised dinner with flatbread and thick chunks of salami. We ate. We were lost. Again. We were surrounded by fireflies. Julie broke into tears.

The next morning, we dropped our packs, as planned, and backtracked to the sink to refill our water bottles. The logic of an historical landscape fell into place. We were hiking an inland archipelago, island-hopping across hammocks, through a seasonally navigable prairie that floods with the summer rains. I could not place us on the map, but the GPS said we were less than a mile from Tatham Mound. We followed the directional arrow—one mile, a half-mile, one-quarter mile away. The LCD display pointed me north, through a barbed-wire fence.

Undeterred by common sense, I held up the bottom wire and coaxed Julie down a sandy road, pocked by feral pigs. We headed toward the sound of airboats, gunning on the river. The display showed Tatham Mound two-tenths of a mile to the east. I looked right, to a thicket of scrub oak and saw palmetto. "I'm not going any further," Julie announced, "I'll mark our position." She walked no further.

I disappeared into the scrub. The arrow pointed due East. The screen said I was closing in: four hundred feet, two hundred feet. I tore through the smilax, a nasty serrated vine with leaves shaped like arrowheads. The saw palmetto sliced my shins. Unable to see through the scrub, I climbed between two dwarf oaks. I recalled what

a nature-writing friend once told me—copperheads like saw palmetto—and I thought about the wild boar tracks in the road. The nearest hospital was hours away. Where the GPS said I should be standing on Tatham Mound, smilax raked across my face. I turned around.

Panic filled the space in my brain, previously curbed with adrenalin. With no path through the scrub, I followed the GPS due west, threading my way through the oak and saw palmetto. My gashed shins started to sting. Julie was nowhere in sight. "Marco," I shouted. A nervous voice answered, "Polo." I traded more exchanges. The voice grew steadily louder and I found my way back to the dirt road. In hindsight, I realized that we had already passed our destination—along some dry prairie a half-mile back, I noted an assuming rise in the scrub oak. (I marked Bachelor's Buttons in my field guide.) But what would I expect to find there? Amateur pot-hunters love to gather arrowheads and ceramic shards. With no spatial-temporal context, these artifacts are worthless. I had no interest in pillaging the "authentic" Florida. Even if I could dial up the past from this swampy landscape, what language would I speak with these ghosts? Timucuan? Miccosukee or Creek? The native-Quechua speaker, El Inca Garcilaso, is clear about the politics of translation.

A plaintive, this-side-of-angry voice cried behind a stand of palmetto: "Tom?!" Julie had not moved for fifteen minutes (she would say thirty), left alone to worry about feral hogs, without a map or directions, trespassing, abandoned by a husband who was nosing around a protected site. I apologized profusely. Julie forgave me. She even let me pause by the prairie that most likely adjoined Tatham Mound.

Our search for De Soto had ended. I could blame my final folly on the now-primitive GPS. I had marked every spot before and during the trip, every archaeological site, the campground we never found, and where we parked our car. But in a final hot pursuit I overlooked the most important coordinate of all. Venturing into the scrub alone, I forgot to flag my wife.

❖ ❖ ❖

Marjorie Stelmach

Fragments of the One True Loss

We will not die in the world we were born to. Things will be lost.
How they came to be lost will be told to prove our unworthiness.

All our stories now are titled, *How It Is We Have Come to This:*
how, on our watch, the waters rose or hordes swept through;

how plague came followed by drought or drought came
followed by plague; how we allowed our children to leave

for the cities. How once, in the time of our testing, a relic was
vouchsafed to us—a remnant of Gethsemane's darkness,

a splinter of lifeline crushed at the foot of the cross,
a halo bone of the risen Christ—and the relic was lost.

In the rueful wake of that failing, we forged a vessel worthy
of immense emptiness, and of course, it was for the grandeur

of this reliquary we found ourselves famous. Whereupon
we smashed it to dust. In the aftermath, there remained to us

only the dark we cupped between folded hands—fragments of
the one true darkness to which we have now withdrawn to brood

on our children—sailing west, seeking Eden. We know
what that search will come to: nothing—a ruined garden, empty

as the lockets in the hollow of their throats holding photos
of our faces, young. We wait for their stories to return to our shores

bearing the beloved names we gave them, each name emptying
even now of its own story, the one that contains the world

we will die in.

Marjorie Stelmach

A Lesson in Depth

after Morris Graves's "Night Bird," watercolor on paper, 1950

The night bird seems an unlikely predator: white,
       entirely—even the eyes, even the beak.

A calligraphic bird, pared to essentials—Egyptian?
       Greek? A creature possible only in profile,

devised for an urn, but prematurely hatched to
       the curvature of time and space.

Eyes opaque. It can't possibly see me.
       Can it see me?

It perches on my sill now, backed by the murk
       of its own howl-shaped shadow, beak bright

as bone. And its bones? Hollow, composed
       of light—and still somehow their density

buckles the landscape. Watch the night bird's
       watchfulness, you'd swear it was advancing

toward a terrible purpose, though not a feather stirs.
       Talons cruel and curved, beak cruel and curved,

and all the glare of earth's cruel curve alive
       in the white frontiers of its eyes.

Come dawn, when I wake to a white enamel
       chalice positioned on the narrow sill, I vow

not to cringe from the ceremony's cutting edge,
       nor will I deny the day's encroaching

three-dimensionality. I'll rise, and it will be
       only for a heartbeat that I'll wonder

how on earth to call it morning.

James Valvis

Behind the Ears

Years after, when he was sick, when dying,
when he had in fact died three times on the table
only to be brought back, his heart jumpstarted
like a battery in one of his old, busted pickups
he worked on with greasy fingers, grime
blackening the tips of his longish fingernails,
my father told me he was sorry, damn sorry,
about the time with the scrub brush and my ears.
It was a Tuesday just before school at St. Paul's
after complaints had been sent home about me
and my ripped uniform pants, smudged shirt,
my hair unkempt too long on my collar.
Yet he focused exclusively on the dirt
behind my ears, pulled me into the bathroom,
grabbed the wire brush he used for his nails,
and began scrubbing the soft skin of my neck.
He scrubbed as if sanding a two-by-four,
holding the back of my head with the free hand,
but the grime remained even as he drew blood.
Only when I cried out did he notice the dirt
behind my ears was instead fine dark hairs.
All his years my father carried this with him.
With other crimes he was able to forgive himself,
convince himself of the justice of those beatings,
but this one nagged him for the injustice,
and so now, dying, he stood before me,
asking forgiveness, holding out his hands
he couldn't get clean no matter how he scrubbed.

Muriel Hasbun, *El altar de mi bisabuelo/ My Great Grandfather's Altar*, from the series *Santos y sombras/ Saints and Shadows*, 1997, gelatin silver print, Smithsonian American Art Museum, Gift of Mr. and Mrs. Charles H. Moore © 1997, Muriel Hasbun. Reproduced courtesy of Museum of Fine Arts, St. Petersburg, from "Our America: The Latino Presence in American Art."

Two Floors above the Dead

Gunther Gosnell stands by the span of windows that takes up much of the living room wall and looks over the moonlit rooftops of the buildings across Main Street, down to the dark gray French Broad River and up the black swells of Piney Ridge.

"On t'other side of Piney Ridge," he says.

He tries both to remember and to forget the dreams of the night. *Accepts all comers*, the man with the moustache said. *Stay in three minutes and win fifty dollars.* He didn't care about the money, thought only that it would be fun. But the monster lifted him until he felt on his face the heat of the big light that dangled overhead. Then he was flying above folding chairs, above laughing and screaming people.

"Them's dreams," he says and turns from the windows, pads across the floor cold with moonlight like snow.

A dim square of light floats just off-center the oval surface of water.

"A bulb out."

The image shatters and scatters in a frenzy until the trickle ends and the square trembles back together.

A sneeze and a fart. Another sneeze and a sniff.

He eats banana with mayonnaise and peanut butter and drinks a glass of buttermilk.

At the windows again, he sips a cup of lukewarm instant coffee, watching the descending day and remembering the mobile home he lived in so long, over there, beyond the ridge line, in the trees above a deep cutback in the narrow two-lane.

His Christmas lights—lights in every room, lights on every outside edge, lights in the yard and in the trees. Lights everywhere. Lights from Halloween to Easter.

"Pretty!"

One New Year's Day when the lights lay dark beneath ash and snow, Granger brought him to live in this place, up two long flights of stairs ascending without a turn from Back Street to the third floor of Mr. Ramsey's funeral home, to two rooms with a bath and a kitchen and so many windows.

"Light."

And the dead people two floors below.

Granger is there now. So still and pale and thin that it doesn't look like Granger. Not like he was back in springtime.

"Gunther," Mr. Ramsey had said, "we need two holes dug tomorrow. One of them's for your brother, God rest him, and if you don't want to dig that one, I understand. I can get somebody else, no problem. You can just dig the one for the Fredericks boy."

As he dresses, he remembers March, not long after the blizzard. Two graves then too—an old woman, an old man. Another short day to dig. Snow still deep on the ground. When Mr. Ramsey buried the old woman who had frozen to death in her house, Gunther dug the grave and, as he always did, sat on his machine at some distance from the hole as the graveside service proceeded. He remembers closing his eyes and thinking that the mild air and the bright sunshine, red through his eyelids, made it difficult to believe that the blizzard had happened. And he said so again and again to the light midday breeze. When he opened his eyes, he saw people looking in his direction, most of them he didn't know, and he thought they must be looking at his beautiful machine. A couple of faces that turned toward him he recognized and named to himself and to the breeze. When he saw Granger, he waved and called, "Hey, Granger!"—then giggled to himself when Granger put a finger to his lips and shook his head.

Those congregated around the grave were going away, and Granger came to him. They shook hands, and without a word other than his name,

"Gunther," Granger dropped heavily to one knee and tied Gunther's work boots.

Granger said some things that Gunther can't remember now as he tries to tie his boots for this day's work—a shorter day than the one in March to dig two graves. Only the last thing Granger said he remembers. Granger took his hand again and gripped it firmly without shaking.

"I love you, Gunther," he said and let go and began to turn away.

Gunther giggled again and nodded his head.

"Thank you," he said. "Thank you."

As he turned to mount his machine, he thought he wanted say something else, but he couldn't at that moment think what it might be.

"I love you too, Granger," he said later, when it was almost dark above the grave of the old man from the college.

"I love you too, Granger," he says again, now, and bends to pick up his coat from the floor.

He pulls his wool cap down tight over his ears and grabs his lunchbox—"Porky's Lunch Wagon"—filled with Moon Pies and the old thermos of cold coffee. Then he goes out the door and descends the stairs past the living and the dead.

❖ ❖ ❖

Before he died, Granger Gosnell requested that Mr. Ramsey not pressure or even encourage Gunther to attend his funeral.

"He won't understand," Granger said. "And he won't sit still for it." He also feared that if Gunther caught hold of the grief that would swell in the church or swirl around the gravesite, he might feel trapped by it—his understanding overwhelmed—and explode into a mindless violence likely to hurt himself and others. "He's a big boy," Granger wheezed. "A dangerous child. Let him watch from his machine. Like he does."

Mr. Ramsey agreed, and the two of them sat quietly, looking through the picture window at the faded November fields and the blue-brown mountains beyond.

❖ ❖ ❖

Gunther lurched out of the large wooden shed atop his Kubota tractor and backhoe. He whipped left on Back Street and then bounced right on Mill, left again at the Main Street traffic light, right again at the bottom of the hill and across the bridge to Piney Ridge. Wearing a bicycle helmet too small for his head, along with goggles and scarf, he pushed the Kubota as fast as it would go through the cutbacks that climbed up toward the ridgeline, his grin wide, his nose and cheeks reddening in the mid-November air.

At the cemetery he found the graves of his grandparents and parents and his sister-in-law Carrie. He stared at a certain spot on the ground and plotted the length and width, no longer needing either measuring tape or wooden form to see the eight-feet-by-three-feet area he would need. His mind took into account the distance between his mother's grave and Carrie's. He would bury Granger between them. The two feet on each side would be close enough, he thought, for Granger to hold the hands of their mother and his wife until he got used to the dark.

Gunther felt happy about that.

He took his sod spade from its rack on the Kubota and set to work, slicing cleanly beneath the grass and laying the sections neatly on the ground to the left, just at the foot of his mother's grave. When he finished, he had a rectangle of bare earth just the right size and exactly parallel with the graves on either side and in line with graves at its head and foot.

He walked into the woods, where a small shed stood among the trees. From this shed he carried back two thick sheets of plywood, which he put on the ground to protect both the tops of the graves and the vaults beneath from the wheels, stabilizers, and weight of the backhoe. Then he rolled it into position and anchored, reversed the seat and began to dig.

❖ ❖ ❖

Sky light gray and full of cold wind, a snow sky still refusing to release the beauty of the first flakes of the season. Faded and browned grass, stiff, trembles as the sky's breath moves across it. Naked trees. Their leaves lie on the ground at their feet, a few still bright with color.

His machine grabs scoopfuls of earth and lifts them to the left, where a mound grows atop the grave of his father.

"Don't drop dirt on Mama," he says.

Reverend Thorn will stand between the hole and Carrie's grave. People who come here will sit or stand on and around Carrie, but that can't be helped. Mr. Ramsey's boys will put down something to protect her from the tramping and poking feet of people and chairs.

Mama watches his work as he digs straight down from the outline he cut in the sod.

Stay inside the lines, little man!

"I will, Mama," he says and smiles at her.

Carrie neither speaks to him nor looks at him. She stands and stares into the deepening hole.

Has Granger took good care of you?

"Yes, Mama." He tells her about the fire at his mobile home and how Granger found him a new place to live.

Who's gonna look after you when Granger's here with us?

"Little sister will," he says.

O Lord, that Ollie.

"Ollie'll help me, Mama, you'll see. Granger says so."

Carrie stands watching as her husband's grave grows deeper and darker.

❖ ❖ ❖

Gunther wanted to speak to Carrie, but he didn't. She had been kind to him during all the time he had known her. Kinder to him than anybody not in the family, maybe even kinder than anybody except his mother. When that big man he was playing with at the county fair had lifted him and thrown him into the third row and broken his body, hurting his mind, too, even more than it had been hurt when he was born, Carrie nursed him until he could be alone again. His mother had cared for everybody else and for him as she could, but Carrie took care of him more.

The grave was finished, and his mother was gone. Carrie had disappeared too, without word or look.

He removed his machine from the dig site and parked it by the cemetery entrance. Then he returned the plywood to the shed, brought back the grass-green tarpaulin with which to cover the naked earth raised from the grave, sat down at the foot of the hole, his feet dangling inside, and ate three Moon Pies.

❖ ❖ ❖

The grave for the Fredericks boy was to be dug in the cemetery adjoining Reverend Thorn's church, so he bounced back toward Runion, waving, as he crossed the bridge, to Mr. Ramsey's two-man crew going to raise the tent top over the newly opened earth up on Piney Ridge.

He whipped into the Southern Missionary Church's parking lot, then slowed and maneuvered gently toward the plot Mr. Ramsey had marked sometime during the morning by planting a small red flag and leaving protective plywood and another tarpaulin. Gunther fixed his machine so that it was ready to dig and then filled the plastic thermos cup with cold coffee and drank it with another Moon Pie while he sighted the outlines of the grave.

* * *

Graveyard of slanted light and air still cold but snowless. People from the graves not easy to see this time of day. They stand around and watch his beautiful machine work. Some faces are familiar to him, but he doesn't know names.

"Mama says I ain't got no common sense is why I don't know people," he says. "There's a boy to be buried here with y'all," he tells them as he digs. "I don't know how come him to die."

These silent townsfolk used to make him nervous when he dug here, shimmering like a sheet of water that isn't really there on a summer highway. Their silence neither mean nor sad. Nor like Carrie's.

"Y'all know my Granger, I bet," he says above the noise of digging. "I just dug him a place over to Piney Ridge."

His machine grabs a scoopful of dirt and lifts it as he watches.

A voice reaches him, and he looks up to see a living man among the dead.

❖ ❖ ❖

"I'm sorry about your brother," Reverend Thorn said again when Gunther shut down the backhoe. "He was a good man."

Gunther removed his wool cap and began working it around and around with his thick fingers.

"Afternoon, Reverend Thorn," he said.

Amos Thorn walked through the crowd of shades and stopped beside the Kubota and stood for a moment looking up at Gunther. Then he turned and looked at the work.

"That's a fine looking grave, Gunther," Thorn said. "Gene Fredericks will appreciate it."

"Thank you. Thank you."

Thorn turned back to Gunther.

"How are you holding up?"

Gunther sat and looked at the barely visible ghosts.

"Are you all right?" Thorn said. "That's what I mean."

"I'm fine, thank you," Gunther said. "Fine, thank you."

"You can talk to me if you need to," Thorn said.

Gunther looked at the sky and figured a couple of hours of good light remained. He needed to finish before the boys arrived to put up the tent, and he needed to be out of the graveyard before sunset.

"Have you seen your sister Ollie?" Thorn asked. "Is she all right?"

Gunther looked directly at Thorn for the first time.

"Yes," he said. "I know Ollie all right. She'll take care of me now." He suppressed a giggle. "Mama don't think she'll be good at it, but she will."

"She had her baby some weeks before Granger passed, didn't she?"

"Yes, yes," Gunther said. "She's got her a girl child name of Rose." He giggled out loud this time. "I call her Rosie, and she ain't no bigger than a nit!" Then he faced the sky and laughed out loud.

"Rose," Thorn said. He seemed ready to say something else but didn't.

Gunther moved to start the engine again.

"You can come to me, Gunther," Thorn said quickly. "If you or Ollie or the baby needs anything, you can come to me."

"Yes, sir," Gunther said. "Yes, sir, Ollie's a strong woman. Full grown." Then he started the engine, looked at the sky, looked at the grave, and resumed his work without further notice of Reverend Amos Thorn.

❖ ❖ ❖

Just after sunset, he returned to the Back Street shed without the usual cleaning of the Kubota's bucket and teeth, its tires and stabilizer pads.

"Hey, Granger, I'm back," he said to the double doors at the foot of the wide stairs.

"Hey, Mr. Ramsey, I'm home," he said to the doors at the middle landing.

He turned on water for a bath and shed his clothes, rinsed his thermos at the tub spigot and set it on the back of the toilet. When the tub was half full he turned off the water and squeezed down into it, his hips squawking against the sides as he settled. He sat still for a long time, thinking nothing.

When he felt the water cooling, he washed his face and hair with soap, rinsed by pouring soapy water from a big plastic NC State cup he kept beside the tub, and pulled the plug.

On the stovetop in the kitchen, he found the soup beans and cornbread Mrs. Ramsey had brought sometime in the afternoon. He stood naked by the table and ate these along with a glass of buttermilk, then went to his chair in the front room and watched the last light drain from the sky above Piney Ridge until he fell asleep.

❖ ❖ ❖

While Gunther slept two floors above the dead in Mr. Ramsey's funeral home, Ollie sat suckling Rose in the kitchen of the house Granger had left her and wondering if she could ever make it her home. She wished she could take the baby and go back to her cabin in Belva, but it had burned to the ground a few weeks after she had moved here in mid summer, already several months pregnant, to take care of Granger. This was the homeplace. This her mother's kitchen and then Carrie's. She hadn't been here often when Carrie ruled, but she could remember her mother moving back and forth through this space, always cooking. They had never gotten along, her mother and she. People had said many times within her hearing that the two of them were too much alike to get along. Ollie still couldn't see that. During slow, silent nights in her cabin, she had come to believe that the chasm between them had opened when Gunther had come home so very wounded, and her mother, Ollie believed, had rejected her in order to care for him.

She was never that close to Granger either, he being almost twenty years older. Even though Carrie and he never had children, he was the golden boy in both family and community, whose birthright seemed stamped on their mother's affection and everything in the house and everywhere in the fields. He had tried to reclaim her as a Gosnell, as a dependent, after their mother died, but she snubbed every effort. They had come to know one another better in his last few months, but not really as brother and sister.

Granger had requested, at the end, that she take care of Gunther. She told him, of course, that she would, but she worried about how seriously to take such a deathbed promise. Gunther frightened her. Only a few years younger than Granger but still several older than she was, he had, from her earliest memories, filled her mother's house with his body and his voice and his energy. Then he was gone for a long time but returned the kind of mammoth simpleton that often haunted the horror shows she watched over the bony shoulders of boys at the Twilight Reel. Her mother welcomed him home as prodigal at the same time that she piecemeal banished Ollie as profligate. Ollie dropped the notion of herself as daughter and little sister and became strong and independent, but now she felt her independence lost in the role of caretaker for first Granger and Rose, now Rose and Gunther. She hoped the strength that had kept her independent for so many years wouldn't abandon her but transform into more of her mother's kind, even though that thought turned her stomach.

The upstairs room Gunther had shared with Granger during much of their boyhood would need some work in order to be made ready for him, but he seemed to be managing well in his little apartment. She need not rush to bring him here, she thought. For now, she could work out a schedule with Mrs. Ramsey so that a few nights every week she and Rose could take supper to Gunther and stay and get to know him better. She could carry in some groceries and maybe cook there from time to time.

The baby stirred and stopped feeding.

Ollie looked down to find Rose not asleep but staring up at her with an intense absence of expression. Once again she tried to discern the color toward which the eyes were tending, but they remained an infant's deep and impenetrable slate blue.

❖ ❖ ❖

Dark again. Ceiling patterned with foreshortened window shapes from streetlights below. Cold room. Cold skin.

Gunther, get your clothes on. It ain't decent nor healthy to sit around naked like that.

Two shades in the shadows in the corners of the room. Granger is one. The other must be the Fredericks boy.

You'll catch your death, little brother.

"No, I won't neither, Granger." He sits and looks at the second shade, a dark outline against the wall and two glittering eyes. "Mikey Fredericks, that's your name." He rubs his belly and leans forward suddenly. "He likes it! Hey, Mikey!" he says and giggles behind his hand.

Don't be scared, Gunther.

"I ain't scared. And don't you be scared neither, Granger. Mama and Carrie is waiting for you." He tells Granger about digging his grave and about seeing their women there, what they did and what he and their mother said, how Carrie hadn't said a word and how he wished she had. "I told Mama Ollie will help me."

Granger stares downward through a window.

You need to get on your pajamas and get in the bed.

"I don't have any pajamas."

Ask Ollie to get you some.

"I will, Granger," he says and smiles at him.

I love you, Gunther.

"Thank you," he says. "Thank you." Then, "I love you too, Granger."

He stands up and stretches, goes to the refrigerator for a few swallows of cold buttermilk, wipes his mouth with the back of his hand, and then disappears into his bedroom without a glance at the shades left lingering in the shadows.

❖ ❖ ❖

With Gunther pacing to and fro in front of the silent backhoe, Ollie was the only immediate family in attendance at the graveside. Mr. Ramsey's oldest son, a thin and serious young man and very much in control of the proceedings, seated her—Rose in arms—in the center of the first of two rows of folding chairs set up for the mourners. Cousins she knew only by name and only because they had visited Granger in his final weeks took the seats on either side of her. Other elderly folks settled into the second row, and a few men stood at random behind.

The vault with its lowering device was positioned over the mouth of the grave, and when all were seated, the pall bearers came shuffling and stamping heavily with the casket between them and maneuvered it onto the lowering device. Then one by one these removed the flowers from their lapels and lay them on top of the casket.

Ollie paid close attention to Gunther, to his movements and the modulations of his voice, watching and listening for signs of distress. Even when Reverend Thorn took his place in front of her and looked down with a nervous smile, she didn't take her eyes from Gunther.

Thorn cleared his throat and, after a moment, began.

"We gather here in this beautiful glade on Five Finger Mountain to commit Granger Gosnell to his final rest between his mother, Sally, and his one true love, Carrie."

Ollie heard a louder but inarticulate sound from Gunther, and she felt those around her start in their seats. Gunther had stopped pacing for the moment and stood staring open-mouthed toward graveside and mourners, and Ollie wondered what, if anything, was in his mind.

"Think of all the changes in the world Granger witnessed since his birth in 1939. My goodness, it's hard to imagine. But what's even harder to imagine is the change he's experiencing now."

"Amen," from one of the standers.

"Although Granger and Carrie, who I'm sorry to say I never met, had no children, he will be long remembered in this community, in his church and in the lives of his family, Ollie and her Rose and—"

❖ ❖ ❖

"—Gunther."

A name. His name. Beneath the cold gray sky, heavy with pendant snow. In the preacher's voice his name shivers among the winter-brown grass.

Gunther. Gunther. Gunther.

In more voices now—Mama's and others'—it rises to echo among the stones and scatter into the woods.

The shades of the dead stand all around in gradations toward invisible in the weak midday light. Over near Ollie stand Carrie and Mama and, yes, Granger, clearer than any.

"Carrie?" he calls.

She looks at him in the way that he remembers waking to see her looking at him as she nursed him through his bad time. Then she turns to Granger, and Granger turns to her.

"Granger, my boots need a tying!"

He lurches forward toward the hole he dug the day before. He sees Ollie looking at him, directly at him, eyes wide as she rises and thrusts Rose into the arms of Preacher Thorn, who looks down at the child as if afraid of such a tiny thing.

"Ain't no bigger than a nit!"

Ollie comes to meet him. Runs in her mother's black dress to meet him.

Then he is on the ground. On his back on the ground. Like when that big man threw him out of the ring and into the third row.

Ollie sprawled on top of him. Somehow holding him down.

"Carrie!"

Ollie says something. Says it again.

Ollie'll take care of you now.

Granger's voice? No, Carrie's.

And he begins to still. Facing a sky without expression.

Against the blank gray above his Ollie. Something. A grayer speck against the gray. Something descends. An angel. A dollop of cloud. Something descends and becomes strangely smaller. And whiter. Descends from the gray sky and past the tops of the naked gray trees. Without haste. It alights in Ollie's black hair, lingers there for a moment, perfect and white against her black hair, grows smaller and then disappears into her.

❖ ❖ ❖

Notes on Contributors

Carlos Almaraz was born in Mexico City in 1949 and grew up in Chicago and Los Angeles. He studied at the University of California, Los Angeles, and later earned a Master of Fine Arts degree from Otis College of Art and Design in 1974. In 1973, Almaraz and three other artists co-founded Los Four, a local art collective whose collaborations brought Chicano street art to the attention of the Los Angeles mainstream art community. Almaraz also created murals, banners, and other artworks for César Chávez and the United Farmworkers Union. Although Almaraz died in 1989, his pastels, paintings, and murals remain a major influence on younger Latino artists. The Los Angeles County Museum of Art will put on the most comprehensive exhibition of his work in 2017.

Bryce Berkowitz's poetry has appeared or is forthcoming in *Passages North, Oyez Review, Oxford Magazine, Evansville Review,* and *Tule Review.*

Charles "Chaz" Bojórquez is a Mexican-American artist who grew up in Los Angeles in the 1950s and '60s. There, he was introduced to the cholo writing, particularly in East Los Angeles, where latino gangs would tag buildings in their neighborhoods to claim their territory. Unlike the bright cartoon-style murals of the East Coast graffiti, cholo writing features stark black-and-white lettering that pays homage to traditional typefaces. Bojórquez created his own style of cholo writing, which he began to tag on the streets throughout the 1970s and '80s. His work is a variation on the classic Gothic, an homage to traditional writing, but with sharp lines and accents. Now 67, Bojórquez continues to work and considers himself one of the oldest living graffiti artists.

María Brito (born María Cristina Brito in 1947 in Havana, Cuba) is a Cuban-American artist specializing in painting, sculpture, and installations. Her inspirations often come from random words that she hears spoken in a certain manner, from objects that she picks up at flea markets, or from common everyday objects. In 1961, Brito entered the United States by way of Operation Peter Pan. She earned her Bachelor of Fine Arts from Florida International University (FIU) in 1978, and in 1979 obtained her Master of Fine Arts from the University of Miami, Coral Gables, Florida. She lives in Florida.

Dorothy Howe Brooks's work has previously appeared in *Atlanta Review, Poet Lore, Poem,* and many other literary magazines. Her second chapbook, *Interstices,* was published by Finishing Line Press in 2009, and a full-length poetry collection, *A Fine Dusting of Brightness,* was published in 2013 by Aldrich Press.

Jack Bushnell is an award-winning children's author and baseball writer. His personal essays, frequently on science and nature, have appeared in various literary journals, and his third book, *Farm Crossing,* was published in 2004. He lives in Wisconsin with his wife and daughter, where he teaches writing at the University of Wisconsin, Eau Claire.

Allison Campbell is a writer and teacher currently living in Southern Mississippi. She is the author of an illustrated collection of prose poems, *Encyclopédie of the Common & Encompassing* (Kore Press, 2016), and her poems and visual art collaborations have appeared in such places as *The Cincinnati Review, Witness, Rattle, Court Green, Harpur Palate,* and *Tammy.* See more at allison-campbell.org.

María Magdalena Campos-Pons is a Cuban-born artist based in Boston. Campos-Pons works primarily in photography, performance, audiovisual media, and sculpture. She is considered a "key figure" among Cuban artists who found their voice in a post-revolutionary Cuba. Her art deals with themes of gender and sexuality, multicultural identity (especially Cuban, Chinese, and Nigerian), Cuban culture, and religion/spirituality (in particular, Roman Catholicism and Santeria).

Michael Amos Cody was born in Sumter, South Carolina, raised in Walnut, North Carolina, and spent the early years of his adult life as a songwriter in Nashville. He now teaches English at East Tennessee State University. His essays, fiction and poetry have appeared in *The Chaffin Journal, The Southern Poetry Anthology* (Vols. VI and VII), *The Nathaniel Hawthorne Review, The Howl, Pisgah Review, Short Story, Yemassee, Potpourri* and *Fury.* His first novel, *Gabriel's Songbook,* will be published this autumn by Pisgah Press. In recent years he has returned to music, releasing the albums *Homecoming* (2012) and *Wonderful Life* (2013).

Carol V. Davis is the author of *Between Storms* (2012). She won the 2007 T. S. Eliot Prize for *Into the Arms of Pushkin: Poems of St. Petersburg.* Twice a Fulbright scholar in Russia, her work has been read on NPR and at the Library of Congress and is in the *Bloomsbury Anthology of Contemporary Jewish American Poetry.* She received a 2015 Barbara Deming grant and is poetry editor of the Los Angeles newspaper, *The Jewish Journal.*

Kelly Fordon is the author of two poetry chapbooks and a novel-in-stories, *Garden for the Blind,* published by Wayne State University Press in April 2015. www.kellyfordon.com.

Scherezade Garcia was born in the Dominican Republic in 1966. She moved to New York City in 1986 to attend Parsons School of Design with a full scholarship and has lived there ever since. Her work frequently evokes memories of faraway home and the hopes and dreams that accompany planting roots in a new land. Garcia's work is included in the Smithsonian Museum of American Art, El Museo del Barrio, The Housatonic Museum of Art, and El Museo de Arte Moderno in Santo Domingo.

Becky Gould Gibson is a poet living in Winston-Salem, North Carolina. She has had work published in journals, anthologies, two chapbooks, and four full-length collections: *First Life* (Emrys Press, 1997), *Need-Fire* (Bright Hill Press Poetry Book Contest, 2007), and *Heading Home* (Main Street Rag, Lena Shull Book Contest, 2014). "The Xanthippe Fragments," thirty-eight poems spoken by the wife of Socrates before her husband's death, is to appear from St. Andrews University Press in 2016. Until her retirement in 2008, Becky taught writing, literature, and Women's Studies at Guilford College.

Thomas Hallock teaches English at the University of South Florida, St. Petersburg. He is the author of several academic studies, and is currently writing a book of nonfiction essays, "A Road Course in American Literature," that explains his love for the American survey. Selections from the "Road Course," with a bibliographic essay for the essay, can be found at www.roadcourse.us.

Muriel Hasbun's expertise as an artist and as an educator focuses on issues of cultural identity and memory. She is the founder of *laberinto projects*, a transnational, cultural memory initiative that fosters contemporary art practices, social inclusion, and dialogue in El Salvador and its diaspora, through exhibitions, art education, artist residencies, and community engagement. She received an MFA in Photography (1989) from George Washington University, where she studied with Ray K. Metzker, and an AB in French Literature (1983), *cum laude*, from Georgetown University. Most recently, Muriel was Professor and Program Head of Photography at the Corcoran School of the Arts and Design at GWU.

Charlotte Innes's poems have appeared in *The Hudson Review*, *The Sewanee Review*, *Rattle*, *The Raintown Review* (including the recent 2015 anthology, *The Best of the Raintown Review*), and other magazines. Some poems have also been anthologized in *The Best American Spiritual Writing for 2006* (Houghton Mifflin) and *Wide Awake: Poets of Los Angeles and Beyond* (Beyond Baroque Books 2015), amongst others. She is the author of two poetry chapbooks, *Licking the Serpent* (2011) and *Reading Ruskin in Los Angeles* (2009), both with Finishing Line Press. Currently, she teaches and tutors students in English and creative writing at schools in and around Los Angeles. Her first book, *Descanso Drive*, will be published by Kelsay Books in 2017.

Marilyn Joy is a retired teacher of Art and English in public and private schools for more than twenty years. Her poetry and prose and have appeared in a number of print publications including *Writers' Journal Magazine*, *Eclipse*, *Stone Voices*, *Viral Cat*, *Lalitamba*, and *Encore* (a publication for winners of the NFSPS annual contest).

Kate Kaplan is a writer living and working in Los Angeles. She graduated from Sarah Lawrence College and the Northeastern University School of Law. Her work has appeared in *The Santa Monica Review*, *Roanoke*, *Folio*, and other publications. She's currently a student in Warren Wilson's MFA program.

Lance Larsen, poet laureate of Utah, has published four poetry collections, most recently *Genius Loci* (Tampa 2013).

He has received a number of awards, including a Pushcart Prize and a fellowship from the National Endowment for the Arts. He is married to Jacqui Larsen, a painter and collage artist, with whom he regularly collaborates. Their teenage daughter, Tessa, is quite sure she wants to be a chemist.

A. Molotkov was born in Russia, moved to the United States in 1990, and switched to writing in English in 1993. His work has been published or is forthcoming in *Kenyon Review*, *Iowa Review*, *Cincinnati Review*, *Raleigh Review*, *Cider Press Review*, *Pif*, *2 River*, and many more. Molotkov has won New Millennium Writings and Koeppel fiction contests, two poetry chapbook contests, and a 2015 Oregon Literary Fellowship. A full-length poetry collection, *The Catalog of Broken Things*, was published by Airlie Press in October 2016. His new translation of a Chekhov story was included by Knopf in their Everyman Series. Visit him at AMolotkov.com

Elisabeth Murawski is the author of *Zorba's Daughter*, which won the 2010 May Swenson Poetry Award, *Moon and Mercury*, and two chapbooks. She was a Hawthornden Fellow in 2008. Her work has appeared in *The Yale Review*, *FIELD*, *Tar River Poetry*, *Alaska Quarterly Review*, and others. She received the 2015 University of Canberra Vice-Chancellor's International Poetry Prize for "Iconic Photo: Lee Miller in Munich, April, 1945."

Derek Palacio's work has appeared in *Puerto del Sol*, *The Pinch* and *Kenyon Review*, and his story "Sugarcane" won a 2013 O. Henry Award. In 2013 Nouvella Books published his novella, *How to Shake the Other Man*, and a debut novel, *The Mortifications*, is forthcoming in 2016 from Tim Duggan Books, an imprint of Crown.

Anne Ray has worked as a waitress, a gardener, an English teacher, and a fishmonger. Her work has appeared in *StoryQuarterly*, *Gettysburg Review*, *Opium*, *LIT*, *Conduit*, *Gulf Coast*, and *Cut Bank*. She is the author of the libretto for "Symposium," a ten-minute opera, a collaboration with composer Oliver Caplan, performed in 2011 by Juventas New Music Ensemble as part of a contemporary opera series. She was a fellow at the MacDowell Colony and the Virginia Center for the Creative Arts, and works on the 18th floor of an office building in lower Manhattan.

Jenna Rindo worked as a pediatric intensive care nurse in hospitals in Virginia, Florida, and Wisconsin, and now teaches English to non-native speakers. Her poems have been published in *Crab Orchard Review*, *Shenandoah*, *American Journal of Nursing*, *Ars Medica*, *Bellingham Review*, *Calyx*, *Poems Memoir Story*, and other journals. She lives with her husband Ron and children in rural Wisconsin where they raise fruit trees, chickens, and a small flock of Shetland sheep.

Anthony Roesch is an architect and writer. He was born in Los Angeles, now lives in the Smoky Mountains with his wife and three dogs. His work has appeared in *Inkwell Journal*, *Tampa Review Online*, and has been a Top-25 finalist several times in *Glimmer Train*'s Fiction Open and Very Short Story Competitions.

Rebecca Givens Rolland previously had fiction published in *Tampa Review Online*. She won the 2011 Dana Award in Short Fiction, and her poems have appeared or are forthcoming in *Witness, Kenyon Review, Cincinnati Review, Gettysburg Review, Georgia Review, Many Mountains Moving, Versal, American Letters & Commentary,* and *Meridian.* Her first book, *The Wreck of Birds,* won the 2011 May Sarton New Hampshire First Book Prize and was published by Bauhan Publishing.

Frank Romero grew up in the culturally mixed, middle-class Los Angeles community of Boyle Heights and was well into his career by the time he developed a consciousness of being a Latino artist. During the height of the Chicano civil rights movement in the early 1970s, as a member of the Chicano artists' group "Los Four," he attained a new, high-profile status in the larger art community. Romero worked as a designer for Charles Eames and A&M Records, and was the design director of the Los Angeles Community Redevelopment Agency when he designed the first section of the Broadway Sidewalk Project. Although he is known as one of L.A.'s foremost muralists, Romero is now primarily a studio artist.

Brook J. Sadler is a philosopher and poet. Her poems can be found in *The Cortland Review, Atlanta Review, Mixitini Matrix, GW Review, The Boiler Journal, Connotation Press, McNeese Review, Chariton Review,* and other places. Her philosophical essays appear in *Philosophy, Journal of Social Philosophy, The Monist, Midwest Studies in Philosophy,* among other journals and books. She lives in Florida and writes wherever she happens to be.

Marjorie Stelmach's most recent volume of poetry is *Without Angels* (Mayapple Press, 2014). Previous volumes include *Bent upon Light* and *A History of Disappearance* (University of Tampa Press). Her first book, *Night Drawings,* was selected by David Ignatow to receive the Marianne Moore Prize, and a selection of her poems received the first Missouri Biennial Award. In addition to *Tampa Review,* her poems have appeared in *American Literary Review, Boulevard, Cincinnati Review, Ellipsis, The Florida Review, The Gettysburg Review, Image, The Iowa Review, Kenyon Review Online, New Letters, Prairie Schooner,* and other magazines, as well as twice on *PoetryDaily.*

Lee Colin Thomas lives and writes in Minneapolis, Minnesota. His poems have appeared in *Poet Lore, Salamander, The Gay and Lesbian Review Worldwide, Water-Stone Review, Midwestern Gothic, Pilgrimage, Narrative Magazine,* and elsewhere. He is online at leecolintomas.net.

James Valvis has placed poems or stories in *Ploughshares, River Styx, Arts & Letters, Nimrod, Rattle, Tar River Poetry, The Sun,* and many others. His poetry was featured in *Verse Daily.* His fiction was chosen for Sundress Best of the Net. His work has also been a finalist for the Asimov's Readers' Award. A former U. S. Army soldier, he lives near Seattle.

Xavier Viramontes was born in Richmond, California. He earned a BFA Degree in Painting from the San Francisco Art Institute and an MA Degree in Printmaking from San Francisco State University. In the 1970s, he worked with the Galeria De La Raza of San Francisco on a number of billboard/mural projects. His work focuses on his life growing up in a Mexican/American household. He touches on rituals and themes that are specific to Latin culture but also addresses universal themes, including matters of life and death. He currently teaches printmaking at City College of San Francisco.

Suzanne Williamson is an American photographer who works in the landscape where layers of human narrative are visible. Her image of an ancient Florida Native American mound in this issue bears witness to the living history of an American monument that has survived cultural conflict, ignorance, and fascination. Her photograph is a reflection in the mirror of that history. Williamson's work has been exhibited nationally in solo and group shows. She received fellowships to the artist colonies, MacDowell and Yaddo, and served on the Board of The MacDowell Colony. Her photographs are in museum and private collections, and have been published or reviewed in *ARTnews, Arts, The Tampa Bay Times, American Archaeology, Harpers, Ohio Magazine,* and *Texas Monthly.* After studying photography at SUNY, College at Purchase, NY and at the International Center of Photography, NYC, she was the Photo Editor of *ARTnews* magazine and recently directed a private photography foundation, Positive Change Can Happen. Currently she provides marketing and mentoring services to artists in Tampa and New York City.

Katherine E. Young is the author of *Day of the Border Guards* (2014 University of Arkansas Miller Williams prize finalist) and two chapbooks of original poetry, and is the translator of *Two Poems* by Inna Kabysh (Artist's Proof Editions). Individual poems have appeared in *The Massachusetts Review, The Iowa Review, Shenandoah,* and *Subtropics.* Young's translations of Russian poets Xenia Emelyanova and Inna Kabysh won third prize in the 2014 and 2011 Joseph Brodsky-Stephen Spender competitions, respectively. More information can be found at http://katherine-young-poet.com/.

❖ ❖ ❖